Into Sight

My Journey From Legally Blind To A World of Clarity & Depth

Into Sig.

My Journey From Legally Bl.
To A World of Clarity & Dept

Pat Vint, LMHC

Any Summer Sunday Books ΔΔΔ Bloomington, IN

ISBN: Print:978-1-953029-01-0;
Ebook 978-1-953029-11-9

Distributed by Ingram. Ebook by Smashwords.

Published by Any Summer Sunday Books, Bloomington, IN
AnySummerSunday.com

About Pat Vint

Pat Vint, LMHC was born blind, gaining some sight at two years of age. She was legally blind into her late twenties, yet obtained a license to drive in her late thirties. She never ceased to strive towards attaining better sight. Her dreams were realized over the past several years with the help of a team of Vision Therapy specialists.

Pat is a retired child and family therapist. She spent her years in practice helping young children, primarily trauma survivors, and their families to heal and thrive. She identifies her life as a therapist as the most rewarding experience in her life.

She lives with her much loved dog, Daisy, in a rural town in Western Massachusetts, a place full of lakes and forests she would never have had the privilege to explore without taking this journey Into Sight.

To order group sets, schedule appearances, or ask questions of Pat, please contact her at Pat@AnySummerSunday.Com

To order sets, contact sales@anySummersunday.com
| Bloomington, IN 47402

Dedication

To Daisy, the little dog who has been my steadfast companion through the highs and lows of writing this book.

Acknowledgements

Heartfelt thanks to Northampton Vision Specialists: Michelle Dilts, my vision therapist for many years, Dr Naomi Clay, my vision therapist, who has pushed me through the last three years of the most tremendous shift in my vision and Dr. Teressa Ruggiero, the mastermind behind treatment which has allowed me to see beyond my wildest dreams. "Into Sight" would not have come to life if my sister Carol had not "badgered" me to tell my story, her word not mine. Steve Schatz, dear friend and writing coach has been my guide who kept telling me that my journey was important and needed to be shared, that the telling would help others who have struggled as I have. He convinced me that I could write, even though he was shepherding a complete novice. And finally an appreciation to David Ellis for the beautiful photos of Monarch butterflies, a precious sight in my new world of depth and clarity.

Preface My Journey

I learned from my parents when I was sixteen years old, that my sight would never be good enough for me to obtain a license to drive a car. I got my driver's license, when I was thirty eight years old. I began my crusade to drive a car when I was thirty three.

For years I had vivid dreams of driving. I would wake from these dreams with the feeling that driving was second nature to me. I marveled that I was even able to parallel park with ease during my nighttime dreaming drives. I kept these dreams and my deeper desire to drive a car to myself, not sharing anything with my husband, friends, and family, I finally mentioned my hidden wish to drive to my therapist, almost as an afterthought, not wanting to give too much importance to this long held secret, not wanting to delve into this dark place of disappointment and loss.

My desire to drive was a complex blend of excitement, dread, and fear. My powerful driving dreams were interspersed with nightmares of car accidents, where my incompetence landed me in prison for vehicular homicide. I had more than poor vision to overcome, to get my driver's license. When I began this challenging, multilayered journey, I had only the support of my therapist, who believed in me and my quest.

My very first driving experience was with this kind, eccentric man. One day, when I arrived at his home office for my session, he met me at the door, car keys in hand. He informed me that we were going for a drive. He "ordered" me to get behind the wheel of his big old American "boat" which lacked a rear view mirror, and off we went. His faith in me convinced me that I could drive a car. I navigated our half hour trip around the small town where he lived with relative ease, considering that I had never before been behind the wheel of a car. I left my first drive with a brilliant smile on my face that stayed with me for many days. I had triumphed.

At the time, my vision was 20/100 with pre-scription lenses. None of the top ophthalmologists in the Philadelphia area, where I grew up, or doctors in Massachusetts, where I later settled, had ever given me any hope or indication that my vision could improve.

Writing this now, I am struck with awe and curiosity: where did I get the "drive" that I could achieve the impossible?

My task was to get my 20/100 vision to 20/60, which would allow me a daytime only driver's license in the state of New York where I was living at the time. I began my search for help outside the realm of modern western medicine.

I spent the next five years seeking help from the alternative healing community, hoping to find practitioners who could address the deficiencies in my vision. I was willing to try anything, so that when my "eclectic" therapist suggested that I meet with a psychic healer whose skills he trusted, I took my skeptical self to her door.

Her office was furnished to create a soft, comforting, atmosphere, not the normal doctor's office to which I was accustomed. After a brief greeting, no forms to be filled out, she ushered me into her treatment room and instructed me to lie down on a massage table. I remember laying in this strange place, feeling the urge to get up and run!

As her hands gently hovered over my body, touching me lightly in places, I remained nervous and cautious. However, I noticed that I felt safe enough, even a bit relaxed. She began to talk to me, sharing her impressions. When her hands reached my head, she rested them there a moment and asked an unusual question. She wanted to know if there had been anything constricting my head when I was two years old. I politely answered in the negative, but the question stayed with me.

Later that evening I called my parents, not mentioning the psychic healer, but asking if my head had been bound with anything, when I was a toddler. By way of explanation, I said I was seeing a new eye doctor who needed this information. I was surprised when my father burst into tears, and began to tell a brand new story about my vision.

Through ragged tears, my father told me that I was born blind and remained without sight until I was two years old. I was thirty-three years old and hearing for the first time that I had been born blind, lived in total and utter darkness as an infant and toddler. He told me that at age two I got my first eyeglasses, a fact of which I was aware. The light pink plastic frame would have felt constricting on the head of a toddler, giving credence to the psychic's "sight". I knew I had been wearing glasses since the age of two, but the rest of the story came as a shock, a blow to who I believed myself to be as a human being. My father continued his tale.

We lived in the suburbs of Philadelphia, so my parents availed themselves of the best eye doctors, who maintained the health of my sightless eyes. During an exam when I was two, my beloved, favorite doc observed that I was responding to light. This was the first time any indication of sight had been noted. He prescribed corrective lenses to see if I could gain more sight.

The tearful conversation with my parents continued, as they tried to reassure me that I grew up as a "normal" child, that my blindness had not led me to be treated differently. They spoke about me as a child who had triumphed over a disability. A disability of which I was never made aware.

I learned in the next few days, in conversations with my older brother and sister, that my blindness was also kept hidden from them. I am still trying to understand how in a family of five, living in a small suburban home, my siblings did not know that their little sister was blind. Imagining my early years as a tiny person without sight is something I will always wonder about. Reflecting on this life-long secret, and trying to piece together the impact on my life took me on a deep inner journey, stirred once again by this writing.

The five years spent trying to improve my vision brought out a discipline and determination in me that proved to be unstoppable. I believed I could repair my eyes and drive. I met many interesting healers along the way. I tried acupuncture, which was scary and painful, but slowed down the Nystagmus a bit. I worked with Meir Schnyder, an Israeli man born with tunnel vision who operated a healing center in California. I went to workshops with him in Massachusetts and had phone consults for about a year. He prescribed hours of deep breathing in a darkened room to relax my eyes, to slow down the shaking from the Nystagmus. I finally landed with Vision Therapy, the system that brought me to the finish line!

As a person who was legally blind into my late twenties, getting my driver's license was an extraordinary, life changing event. I gained independence, which gave me a sense of freedom I had never had, but my vision had not changed significantly, in several key areas. My vision deficits continued to interfere with my quality of life, and driving, although a great improvement in my life, was very challenging.

Driving gave me the power to come and go as I pleased, reducing my dependency on other people. I soon discovered there was a catch: I was extremely frightened, most of the time, I was behind the wheel. My two most debilitating vision problems – Nystagmus and Monocular vision – remained unchanged. These conditions made driving a car much more difficult than for the average person.

When the Nystagmus was activated, my ability to focus diminished and I would often feel forced to pull off the road until my vision settled down, cleared, and I could once again focus properly. Bright light activates Nystagmus, so driving on bright sunny days felt almost impossible at times. Anxiety also intensifies Nystagmus, so when the Nystagmus destabilized my vision and my nerves kicked in, my vision worsened. It took a huge effort to relax enough to get my eyes to return to "normal" so I could get back on the road.

Note: Nystagmus is a constant shaking of the eyes leading to intermittent lack of focus. In my case, this often felt like a freezing or momentary paralysis of my eyes. Monocular vision occurs when the eyes operate independently of one another and are not able to focus on the same thing together, unlike binocular vision, where the eyes work together. Depth perception is possible only when a person has developed binocular vision.

The absence of depth perception while driving a car creates difficulties for which accommodations must be made. For example, prior to developing some depth perception, at a busy intersection I drive through on occasion, I could not determine how to navigate around a medial strip, because the road beyond and the strip appeared flat. Once I had some depth perception the problem was resolved and I knew exactly where to steer my car to safely avoid oncoming traffic.

The Nystagmus was eliminated in February 2018 when I went through a treatment called MST. In February 2019, the addition of prisms into my prescription lenses, enabled me to see in three dimensions for the first time. I do not have total depth perception yet, but I have enough three dimensional sight to make a huge difference in driving a car and other activities requiring depth perception.

An unexpected benefit of the prisms was a dramatic increase in clarity in my visual field. This high definition sight was a huge shock, which took some time to integrate. These improvements to my sight have changed my life in many surprising ways.

My enhanced vision has had a positive impact in areas that one might not expect with a shift in vision. I have experienced changes in the areas of emotional, social, psychological and cognitive function.

I am better able to understand, and describe the impact of my visual problems now that my vision is much improved. I have thought a lot about why this is true and I believe it is because I was so habituated to limited vision, that the difficulties were just assimilated into my life experience. The blur of my world was normal, I did not know there was a clear world or a three dimensional world that I was missing. I knew no different.

When my visual world suddenly became clear, sharp, sparkly, and brilliant in color, I was stunned. I found myself feeling suddenly more awake, alert, seeing so many things for the very first time.

I saw my first spring buds ripening on the trees. This led me to look further and I realized that I was able to follow the birds from the bird-feeder where they plucked seeds, up into the trees where they flew with their treasure. I watched them staring down at me from their perches on high, instead of them appearing and disappearing, like a mirage. I felt like a child making discoveries. I was more curious and I became aware of how I have not explored so many things in nature because I knew it was impossible for me to see more. My broader view of the world opened up my mind as well.

I also began to observe a greater clarity in my thinking. I realized I was making decisions more rapidly, and considering more options in problem solving. My brain was looking around, and seeing more, mirroring my eyes.

I was blind at birth. There was some sight at two. My impairment was first revealed at sixteen. At thirty eight, I finally was given a driver's license. And in my mid-60's I finally began to see the world.

What follows is a collection of my journal entries during my journey into sight.

2/11/2018 Play Ball!

The first time I remember anyone believing that I could see better was in my early twenties. My husband Alan, felt that I could see more if I was taught to use my eyes more effectively. One warm sunny day, he decided that it was time for me to learn how to catch a tennis ball. Up until that time, I had only been able to manage catching a sphere that was basketball size. This limitation was a huge impediment throughout my childhood.

When I was in middle school, I hated the arrival of Spring. The season of rebirth harkened the beginning of the dreaded softball season. I knew that once again, I would be stuck in the outfield, during gym class, assigned the task of catching balls, hit in my direction. No one knew how scared I was out there. I was afraid that one day I would get hit hard by an unseen fly ball. I did a pantomime of a person running to catch a ball, whenever my teammates started yelling that a ball was coming my way. The sad truth was that I could not see the batter hitting the ball so finding a ball, that was just a phantom spec in the sky, was never going to happen.

Back to my parents backyard. There I was, standing across from my best friend/young husband, who was tossing me tennis balls, imploring me to follow the ball with my eyes. The concept was foreign. Alan continued patiently throwing balls that bounced, and rolled all around me, for quite a long time. I can still remember the feeling of shock, and amazement when I finally caught a ball, and held the small round treasure in my hands. It was a feeling of awe and joy that spread through my entire body. As we continued to play I grew to love the experience of watching the ball leave Alan's hand, drifting through the air between us, to fall softly into my own outstretched hands. We played for a long time, until catching became something I did with ease.

Learning to catch came into play, later in life in my work as a child and family therapist. Kids like to play catch, a lot. I became a therapist in my fifties, and hadn't worked too much on my catching game, since my twenties. Miraculously I remembered how to catch. I smiled and smiled, each time I caught a ball thrown to me by a little person, not getting nearly as excited when they caught the ball. These games of catch were all about me. The kids simply enjoyed a game that was their birthright, a right I didn't get until mid-life.

2/11/2018 Maiden Voyage

Driving a car was the only motivation I had for working to improve my vision. I fantasized about the freedom of driving. I saw myself behind the wheel of a sporty little car like the one I had planned to buy from my big brother when I was sixteen, when I was told that I would never drive. I could feel the leather seat beneath me, the steering wheel held solidly in my hands. At night while I slept, I dreamed of driving with ease, fearless, confident in myself behind the wheel. I was in my thirties and tired of begging people for rides, worn down and out by the feeling of being beholden to others. I hated the ordeal of public transportation. I hated living my life by the schedules of other people. I wanted my own independent life. Driving a car was my key to opening the door to a new life.

The impetus to achieve my goal came from a psychotherapist I met with in my thirties. We spoke often about my wish to drive, and my fear of fate punishing me if I ever succeeded. His advice was that I should face my fear and get out on the road.

I arrived one morning for our session to find him standing at the door, car keys in hand. He directed me to sit in the driver's seat of his old American boat of a car, which had lost its rear view mirror. He showed me how to place the key in the ignition, start the vehicle and off we went.

I had no learners' permit, had never sat behind the wheel of a car in my thirty-three years. I wasn't half bad. My therapist guided me into the town of Lenox, around town, through Tanglewood - the home of the Boston Symphony Orchestra - and back to his home office. I felt exhilarated, successful and relieved. No accident, no bodies left behind.

The Secret

At the age of thirty-three, I discovered that my life had started in darkness and I had been slowly, very slowly coming into sight since I was a baby. I have no factual information about the development of my vision as a child. My Mom could only recall me behaving like a normal baby, not needing any special care. She spoke with pride about how well I managed as an infant and later on in school fending for myself, moving my desk close to the blackboard without any help from my teacher.

My memories of my early vision are also limited. I bumped into walls and other hard objects which left bruises. I didn't have any sense of what I was not seeing, except for the blackboard and when my best friend identified the person I saw up ahead of us on our walk home one day, as just a white mailbox. The only memory I have of my sight taking a leap was when I was in my late teens or early twenties when I tried wearing contact lenses. I recall the magic of seeing blades of glass for the first time and sharing this joy with my big sister Carol. Unfortunately the contact lenses became impossible to wear due to my severe astigmatism. There were no more major changes in my sight until my mission to drive began when I was thirty-three years old.

About Nystagmus

Nystagmus is the condition that causes my eyes to constantly shake. I was born with Ocular Albinism. Nystagmus is related to this condition. The rapid eye movements of Nystagmus cause the eyes to lose the ability to focus. The primary triggers are anxiety, stress and bright light. Symptoms occur without warning and sometimes when the aforementioned triggers are absent.

I did not know that my eyes shook until I was a teenager. A close friend noticed my eyes darting around and asked why my eyes moved like this. I felt flustered, embarrassed and shrugged off a response. The realization that the rapid eye movements interfered with my ability to see did not become evident until I was thirty-eight years old and learned to drive. I noticed then that I had difficulty seeing well in bright sunlight. My eye doctor at the time told me the condition was activated by bright light. Until then I had no knowledge of this problem that had so much control over my vision.

I was told by my eye doctors that Nystagmus is a fixed neurological condition, that my eyes would never change. That notion shifted in my late twenties when I was a participant at a week-long training for psychotherapists on the teachings of Gestalt Therapy.

Part of the course necessitated participants taking turns conducting short therapy sessions with one another in front of the group, getting feedback and supervision from the facilitators. The process is called "Working in a Fishbowl", as the people in the center are exposed and vulnerable, seen by all. Our teachers also worked with participants to demonstrate therapeutic intervention. I volunteered to be a client with one of the teachers. I sat across from the trainer and began talking. Before I got too far into my story he noticed the movement in my eyes and demanded that I stop them from shaking. He told me that he had no interest in speaking with me until I could look him in the eye directly! I had never been able to make eye contact due to the Nystagmus. I explained to him that I had no control over my wobbly eyes. He told me that I was making a choice to avoid eye contact. His arrogance was a shaming shock and I broke down in tears. I became angry and cried while the group sat in silence.

I do not turn away from a challenge, so despite my intense emotions I tried to relax my eyes. I managed to achieve the impossible. For the first time in my life, I halted the frenetic dance of my wayward eyes. Mr. Arrogance allowed the session to continue. I do not remember any part of the conversation with this man. He had nothing to say that made a difference. However, I will always remember this short lived triumph. I knew I was able to steady my eyes, although I still did not know how I achieved it. That was forty years ago and trying to steady my eyes continues to be a challenge I face.

Stepping back for a moment, I want to share how Nystagmus affects my vision. When the Nystagmus is active, I feel like I am looking at the world from under water, or through thick walls of glass that separate me from everything outside, like a glass prison. My eyes freeze in what feels like a paralysis. My eyes lose their ability to focus. The harder I try to gain control over my eyes the more intractable they become. Imagine being behind the wheel of a car and suddenly losing the ability to use your eyes to see where you are going. This terrifying experience would force me to get out of traffic immediately and wait until my eyes relaxed enough to regain their ability to focus.

Nystagmus has also interfered with my interpersonal experiences. I am unable to make eye contact. I invite the reader to take a pause here, to imagine not being capable of gazing into the eyes of another human being. I am missing the intimacy that people share through the deep connection we get from looking into the eyes of another person. I give the impression that I prefer distance as I turn my eyes away yet I seek closeness.

Nystagmus is more difficult than other vision problems in part due to its unpredictable nature. Specific stimuli activate the condition but there is no way to know how intense the trigger must be to create a full blown "attack" of out of control eye movement. I also have no control over the movement, which brings on feelings of helplessness and fear. Although shaking eyes can be seen by others, no one knows that my vision has become compromised and that I am fighting for sight and emotional balance. I feel at once vulnerable and a need to regain focus and composure ASAP. The pressure is enormous and stimulates the Nystagmus making the situation I find myself in much worse.

Inside MST

I had mixed feelings about trying Multi Sensory Training. First, there was no guarantee from Dr. Ruggiero that the treatment would have a major positive impact on my vision. The primary reason behind implementing this process was to decrease the shaking of my eyes caused by the Nystagmus. I only had her professional opinion and experience to give me hope.

Second, the treatment would involve twelve consecutive long drives to Northampton. When Dr. Ruggiero advised that I find someone to drive me to the treatments, I felt relieved. She said the treatment would be more successful if my visual system was not stressed beforehand. My good friend George made the treatment possible by agreeing to drive me to the sessions. I am grateful to George who did so much more than shepherd me back and forth between my home and the office during the MST.

When I arrived for my first treatment, I was ushered downstairs into the basement of the vision center where the MST sessions would take place. A technician would be my guide throughout the sessions. I was nervous as I entered the treatment room. The technician explained how each session would proceed.

At the beginning of each session, I lay down on a massage type table in the center of the room. During the session, the table moved in ellipses that lifted me sixteen inches into the air. The direction of the rotations shifted 180 degrees on alternate days. While the table moved, I gazed at a light placed above my head. As the table moved the distance of the light varied from 14 to 30 inches away from my eyes. Colored filters ranging from magenta, red, blue, turquoise, and green were placed over the bright light on a schedule determined by Dr. Ruggiero. Additionally, I listened to a cacophony of discordant "music" through headphones.

The sessions took place in a pitch dark room. Each session was divided into two parts with a ten minute break. During the break the technician presented an eye movement vision therapy exercise to ascertain any changes in my eyes, particularly in the Nystagmus.

When the first session began, another disturbing component emerged. The motor that moved the table was very loud and the table vibrated. I was frightened, filled with a sense of dread that I could not tolerate the entire session and certainly would not be able to manage eleven subsequent sessions. The "music" was another irritating and unsettling aspect. The comfort provided by the technician and a lot of deep breathing got me through the first half of the session. Although I was quite shaken and had a touch of vertigo, I agreed to continue the process after the break.

When the entire session was over, my balance was so compromised that I needed assistance to walk up the stairs.

I was nervous about continuing the treatments, but my drive to improve my sight urged me onward. The next session was difficult, but I began to adjust to the horrible motor noise and the stress of the sensory overload lessened. My reward was that during each break, when my eyes were tested, the technician noticed that the

Nystagmus eye movements were slowing down gradually.

I was exhausted after each session and realized I needed to cancel work and my daily routine. For twelve days, I went to MST, ate , slept and cuddled with my little dog. By the end of the twelfth session, the technician told me my eyes barely shook. Over the next couple weeks when I arrived for vision therapy my vision therapist Dr Clay confirmed that the Nystagmus was no longer visible.

It took weeks for me to believe that the Nystagmus had been eradicated and much longer to feel safe enough to relax in the knowledge that I had control over my eyes at last.

3/21/2018 The Aftermath

It has been a month since the MST treatment eradicated my Nystagmus. Finally my eyes are steady. They no longer shake. I am in control. Even when I am nervous my eyes focus. Since the treatment, I have been in a state of celebration. However, over the past several days something has shifted. I am now steeped in sadness, confused to have fallen into this dark place.

My life is no longer a scary experience of living with eyes that would betray me without notice, freezing if they sensed I was a bit nervous or on edge or if the sun became too bright.

No longer will I be talking with a person and suddenly have my eyes become stuck and go out of focus, leaving me frightened , feeling like a fool who should never make eye contact for fear of this happening. Now I can look right into someone's eyes while I speak to them. My eyes are steady like a rock.

I feel like a normal human being. I no longer have this bizarre abnormality that made me look and feel deformed. There is nothing wrong with me, nothing broken anymore.

Nobody knows how I felt living in the world, how I had to hide from the eyes of other people. Almost sixty-seven years living like this and then in twelve days, I break into a new world. I look boldly at people now when we meet.

I am able to gaze into the eyes of another human being knowing that I no longer look strange without having to avert my crazy shaking eyes. Can anyone really imagine how I feel? Who can possibly understand?

Perhaps this deep sadness is arising from all the years I lived in fear.

5/2018 A Still Life

Doc said I have a unique story to tell. Life without Nystagmus from someone who has lived with the shaky eyes for sixty-six years. I am a rare person who has lived in both worlds. I have lived with the shaky eyes my entire life and now they are still.

The world I see is so much more beautiful than the one I lived in just a few months ago. I am often overwhelmed with emotion, unable to take lightly the stunning nature of the visual changes. And Doc Theresa said it is here to stay. My eyes are now steady. They will not start shaking again. Perhaps that is the most startling thing. This new world is mine, maybe forever? Could be.

Images being still means that they are clear, have depth, more color, texture, shadow and light. Faces have contours and wrinkles. Eye contact can be held. A person can be really looked at and seen, studied, known. Relationships change, deepen, when one sees another person clearly. There is no mask, fog, film, keeping me from the Other.

7/24/2018

I spent all of my life navigating a world that could freeze at any moment. I used to look at something .a person's face, a sun dappled road, and the image would freeze right before my eyes. I would try to focus, try to clear my vision, move my eyes, and they simply would not move. They remained fixed no matter what I did. I would breathe, try to relax, pull off the road if I was driving. If talking to someone, I would look away, breathe, try to get a grip on my very frightened self.

I do not know if anyone understood what I experienced. The eye doctors I have seen over many years listed Nystagmus as one of my eye disorders, but they didn't talk to me about how the rapid movement of my eyes affected my sight. I didn't even understand my experience completely until the Nystagmus was gone. I knew that my eyes would suddenly feel stuck, that I couldn't see whatever I was trying to focus on. Occasionally a friend would tell me my eyes were moving real fast, but I could not see this in the mirror as hard as I tried to catch the rapid movement.

Now my eyes move freely, focusing on the object of my attention. I am in charge of my eyes instead of my vision being shut down by the Nystagmus. My eyes no longer freeze. They do not get stuck. I am not suddenly blinded by dappling sunlight on a country road. I am able to see, my world feels wide open, expansive.

8/1/2018

It is only now that the Nystagmus is gone that I know how much it impaired my vision. I am often filled with joy, appreciating my newfound sight without Nystagmus. Then I plummet into the pain of memory, the horrible grief, the loss, the pain of what my life was like. My life is now divided into "before and after Nystagmus". The change is that dramatic.

There is a recurring experience of seeing something clearly and immediately remembering the physical feeling of my eyes feeling stuck when the Nystagmus was activated. I did not know how to articulate the experience until it no longer existed or how strong the impact was, until it was gone. The Nystagmus had a life of its own. I had no power over it. I did not know that the Nystagmus was the cause of my eyes losing the capacity to focus. I stopped trying to make my eyes focus. I gave up. Resignation was demoralizing and painful.

Now as I adapt to my steady eyes I am aware of sharper focus , brighter and more vivid colors. My eyes seem to be open wider as if searching for details instead of not trying to see.

2/20/2018 The Facts

I know now how my severely compromised vision influenced all aspects of my life. My lack of awareness of my disability throughout my life is like a deep well of muddied water that holds secrets about myself which I hope to one day see more clearly. I became more conscious of the severe impact of my impaired vision only after my vision improved dramatically beginning in early 2018.

I was sixteen when I was first confronted with the reality that something was terribly wrong with my vision, that I was not merely near-sighted, as I had always thought. I was planning to buy my big brother's tiny red car that he had outgrown, so I would have a car to drive when I got my license. One day around my sixteenth birthday my parents sat me down and told me that I would never see well enough to drive a car. They went on to explain that the state approached them every year urging them to enroll me in the local school for the blind. This was just the beginning of a saga of sad parental tales about my poor vision, but I paid little attention only taking in the words "you can't drive".

My life went on. The story of my vision and driving went on "pause" for seventeen years, until I was thirty-three years old. I thought I had let go of my wish to get a driver's license. However, often when I slept, I dreamed about driving. In dreams I practiced parallel parking until I was a pro! I imagine that I practiced in my sleep what I soaked in though osmosis from hours spent being driven around by my Mom.

I got behind the wheel of a car when I was thirty-three years old. I didn't even have a driver's permit. I did have a very good, gutsy therapist who wanted me to get a taste of my dream. He put me in his big old American boat and directed me around Lenox, MA. I liked it! I didn't hit anything. The police didn't arrest me. Nothing bad happened. I was on my way to get my driver's license. It took another five years. When I turned thirty-eight I got my first driver's license in the state of New York because their requirements were less stringent.

Let me take a moment to explain how the terms Blind and Legally Blind entered my world view. My parents tale about the school district trying to place me in the school for the blind got lost in my grief about the loss of my dream of driving. I did not give the Blind word another thought until I was thirty three and my father informed me I had been totally blind until I was two years old. I later learned that my visual acuity of 20/200 which I had until I was almost thirty years old classified me as a legally blind person.

After learning about my blindness at birth I knew that I needed more information. I wanted the true story about the mystery of my eyes. I sought out a geneticist to see if I could learn more about the root cause of my vision problems. He gave me the diagnosis of Ocular Albinism and explained that the minuscule amount of pigment in my eyes caused the Nystagmus and other deficiencies.

Much later in my life, in 2019, I learned from my brother's wife, that I was also born about six weeks prematurely and that I spent the first week of my life under ultraviolet lights. It is common knowledge that a premature birth can have a negative impact on vision so I was curious about my birth. I had inquired about a premature birth repeatedly but had always been told by my Mom that I was carried to full term and had a normal birth. I believe this story is how my Mom remembers my infancy in her heart and mind and not a secret she was trying to keep.

2/25/2018 Coming Out

I never told anyone that I had a problem with my vision. I would not admit to not being able to identify something in the distance pointed out by a friend. I smiled and nodded my head in false appreciation, always fearful of being revealed as an impostor.

This memory brings me back to being scared and lonely in the school cafeteria. I couldn't see my friends to go and sit with them and it was too unsettling to walk around the entire room looking closely at the crowd of kids to identify people I knew. I didn't want to stand out so I just faked being fine sitting wherever I could find a seat. I never asked anyone to help me. And none of the teachers asked if I needed help. My poor vision was an invisible problem that I lived with alone.

The first time I ever told anyone that I had poor vision was when I worked as a clinician in a residential treatment center for adolescent girts, trauma survivors. I remember the exact moment clearly. Two big strapping girls were walking quickly towards me up a hill on campus. Many of the girls could become violent with unknown provocation and I feared that if I didn't greet them by name they might feel hurt, offended and lash out. I remember calling out to them that I could not see who they were. I feel the immense release I felt at that moment as I write these lines. I was also aware that we shared being broken and there was a comfort in letting them into my world of shadows and darkness.

2/28/2018 The Spinning Chair

A while ago my doctor suggested an eye exercise which required an office desk chair that could spin. Living in a people-friendly small town in the Berkshires, I managed to have a spinning chair delivered to my door by one of many generous neighbors the day after I learned I needed this new piece of "equipment."

Why a spinning chair? Dr Ruggiero had attended a conference where she learned of new eye exercises to treat Nystagmus, the first of their kind. She wanted my vision therapist, Dr. Clay, to work with me on these new exercises. Part one of the exercise was to create a state of dizziness in the patient. This brings on an attack of Nystagmus (the uncontrolled eye movement). The patient is then instructed to read a letter chart while the eyes are moving. The goal of the exercise is to teach the brain to adapt to the eye movement which should result in the movement slowing and then stopping.

In my next Vision Therapy session with Dr Clay, we worked on the spinning exercise. I first sat in a swivel desk chair and spun until I was dizzy, stopped and read a chart of colored shapes and numbers. I did this four or five times. Then feeling ill, dizzy and miserable, I ended the session and my friend drove me home. I could barely walk on my own. I persisted with this exercise at home for weeks, making myself dizzy and nauseous each morning, hoping to learn to still my wild eyes.

The motivation to do the spinning exercise day after day came from my friend George who often drove me to Vision Therapy, which was a long distance from my home. He supported me when I struggled and rejoiced in my little victories. One day sitting across from one another at my kitchen table he asked me to look at him. I did as he asked and after several moments he said "your eyes are totally steady and when you used to look at me they moved a lot."

Despite the sheer joy of succeeding in beginning to tame my unruly eyes I decided to halt the spinning chair exercise. I was simply suffering too much. I was discouraged, but continued my journey into sight.

3/4/2018 My Sister Carol

Carol is my big sister, six years my elder. She has been my cheerleader and constant support throughout my vision quest. We were both shocked to learn in my thirties that I spent my first two years on earth totally blind, in darkness. I believe the news stunned her just as much as it shook me. When I am crying for joy about a vision breakthrough her excitement mirrors my own. I feel her walking beside me on this path to clearer sight even though she lives a day's train ride away. She is the person I trust to understand and share my experience. Carol often reminds me how difficult and "heroic" my journey has been. Her admiration empowers and urges me forwards when the work is hard and I am discouraged. We celebrate my victories together.

3/5/2018 Bumping Into Walls

I used to bang into walls, trees, car doors, furniture and even "clothes-lined" myself a number of times. These common run-ins didn't bother me too much. They were just part of my daily life and did not seem unusual until I was probably in my mid thirties. I was used to slamming my head, leaving large bumps and bruises, sometimes feeling a bit unsteady like I might pass out. I did not attribute my "clumsiness" to my poor vision. I felt clumsy and stupid for not seeing enough to avoid collisions.

About a year ago I began to think that maybe vision therapy could be directed at helping me not to bang into things. Since then, Dr Ruggiero has adjusted my exercise regimen, which has made a big improvement.

I have also begun to slow down! I have always moved at a fast, nearly frenetic pace. My new found dedication to meditation helped me reduce the speed at which I physically navigate my surroundings. The combination has been successful. No more lumps and bumps! I feel safer in the world. A huge relief.

3/22/2018 Tiny Miracle

Last night a miracle happened in my quest. I invited a friend to look straight into my eyes and then asked if they were moving and they were steady!!! My friend Steve told me he just watched my eyes in awe. I have always hidden my eyes from people, never really looking at them or letting them look into my eyes. I was so guarded for good reason. I imagined my eyes must have looked freakish, scurrying around in their sockets, like little mice trying to escape.

3/24/2018 Sun on Snow

Today was the **March for Our Lives** in support of gun safety and I went to support the kids and myself. The ride home along Kirchner Road was gorgeous. Bright sun shining on glistening snow, barren trees . beautiful silhouettes. Endless blue sky, a beautiful experience after the sadness of the March. I loved the clarity of the scene. I marveled at the juxtaposition of this experience compared to my usual driving experience on a day like this.

I used to dread sunny days in winter when I needed to go somewhere in my car. Nystagmus responds badly to bright light. One could say these conditions raise Nystagmus to its heights. The visual world goes crazy. Eyes shake wildly, making focusing random at best. Eyes freeze, stressed, struggling to bring life into focus. Terror is the feeling that comes with this when one is driving a car. But not on this day. Nystagmus no longer rules. I am free to rejoice in the beauty of sun on snow.

4/3/2018 Vision Journal

Saturday I got lost due to a detour. A nasty driver got behind me and was tailgating and blasting his big, fat, loud, truck horn. I was afraid he might run me off the road. It was a bright sunny day, the worst for Nystagmus, but my eyes did not shake at all. They were tired and strained after the short ordeal, but held steady and focused.

The Sunday before that, I was coming back from helping friends move into their new home and I saw an entire vista of the Berkshire Hills that I had never seen before on Route 20, a familiar roadway I have traveled for many years.

This past Saturday, I was driving home from West Stockbridge and I saw a lake for the first time. I must have gone by it hundreds of times when I lived in Richmond, never seeing the sparkling blue water until today.

Last night over dinner, my friend George noted that my eyes do not move randomly any more. The fact that people who see me a lot are now aware that my eyes can look into theirs with ease is the best.

There is so much joy for me in this experience with my eyes. Joy has never been a word I associated with my vision.

I feel so much happier with my brand new eyes. Just about every day there is something new that I see with more clarity. I seem to be noticing and reading more road signs lately, too. It is quite helpful in finding my way.

4/9/2018 Snippets

Waiting for my young therapy client to arrive at my home, I find myself sliding down a slippery slope of anxiety, a feeling of being lost and a bit of depression.

Then I realize that I am worried about tomorrow -- a long drive to Great Barrington and then working until 7:00 at night. Writing this down eases the fear as I remind myself that my eyes are better and I can relax about the drive. I return my attention to sitting in my kitchen listening to the little dog gently woofing her displeasure at not being outside and perhaps being on leash, suspecting maybe that I am going to keep her and her wild antics outside and away from my young guest when she arrives.

Then I recall an awareness of my new vision. Every day I see something new. A couple of days ago, I realized that in my woods now I can see the wall that is hidden behind all the brush from the trees that were taken down a few years ago. I traced the entire length of it with my eyes, happy to finally see this wall that marks my path around my woodland sanctuary. I saw the wall again on my walk today ... now commonplace, but still a great joy.

4/10/2018

Listening to Irish jigs and happy with the little dog. Light snow covering everything -- so pretty even in April! But the anxiety is alive and well inside this morning and is disturbing my gut. Stay in the moment, here with all the beauty around me. Just keep staying present and see what happens OK? Pretty, pretty snow. Yes I can see much more of everything now.

Just an hour later the depression comes, or maybe it is just sadness? I need to see what is going on right here right now around me. I feel anxious about driving to Great Barrington and the busy day ahead of me with perhaps too many appointments. But nothing to do about it now except do it as well as I can. I don't have to be a super star every minute and it's OK if I am a little late this afternoon. I have to take enough time in between sessions to regroup and catch my breath. I see so much better now that I shouldn't be all anxious about the drive, but I am. I don't know if it's habit or what. Maybe just so many difficult drives keep the worried feeling in my body and I have to catch up with my new experience I guess.

4/2018 Snippet

And now the pain of feeling and remembering a life of straining to see, pretending to see. Isolated, silently watching, looking for clues to decipher that which is in plain sight to others. "Don't you see that?" "It's right there in front of you!" What's wrong with you? The unspoken statement she heard from a changing crowd of one.

4/18/2018 Talking With My Big Brother

The other day I called my big brother Mike and told him in a deeper way what it means for me to have my eyes suddenly steady, not shaking. I still wonder if the Nystagmus is in a kind of remission or gone? He told me that he remembered when we were kids seeing my eyes shaking all the time, and wondering how I could ever see anything with my eyes moving like that. His statement shocked me.

I realized that nobody in my entire family had ever mentioned anything about the movement in my eyes, and nothing about my limited vision. Not a single word in my entire life with the family! Nothing was talked about until I started working to get more sight. I did it all on my own. In fact, nobody in my life ever spoke of my shaking eyes until the teacher in a clinical training workshop I was attending DEMANDED that I make my eyes stop moving (see entry on February 14, 2018). He would not even speak to me until I made them stop. And somehow, that day, I managed to slow them down enough so that he noticed and we had our conversation, which of course I cannot remember. He is quite memorable because he believed in my sight and my capacity to see.

4/19/2018 Woodland Sightings

Along the path Daisy and I walk every day I happened upon a huge boulder I had never seen before, as if it had been placed along my path just the other day instead of resting there for hundreds of years. Another bewildering sight. I expanded my gaze to include the craggy moss covered rocks which form the old farm wall that surrounds our wood, luscious dark green against the April snow.

More important, at least to the little dog, is that I have learned over the past few days how to throw sticks that travel a distance, instead of blindly throwing sticks that tangle up on branches, and hang in the trees. I now have the ability to look and SEE a clear path through the dense woods and throw sticks unimpeded so they are worth the chase for my sweet four legged companion. Little victory fulfilling a big dream.

4/22/2018 First Sightings

Matchbox cars sparkling in the sun, gliding along built-to-scale highways. Hundreds of houses in neat little rows. HO trains running along their tracks. Barbie Doll swimming pools. Miniature football field. A child's world seen for the first time by this grown woman looking out the window of an airplane, giggling with delight. I have flown many times and gazed down at the ground as a plane descended closer and closer to land and enjoyed the colors of earth, sea and sky mountains in the distance. Aware of the blur of neighborhoods, snaking rivers and roads. Not much to draw my attention, until now.

5/2/2018

Today was a hard day. I have been panicked about driving to the train to Hudson and haven't been able to figure out why. Perhaps I am remembering the terrifying times I made the drive and could not see through the blur of my shaking eyes. Talking with my sister Carol just now by phone about my fear, she shared an image of something being peeled away, leaving me exposed.

This new sight leaves me feeling emotionally raw at times. I feel oddly exposed. Carol spoke about the physiology of my experience and this I understood. I am not just having emotional responses to the horrible memories of not seeing, my eyes freezing, feeling half blind as I tried to drive a car and struggling to see into the eyes of another human being. There is more going on than that.

5/9/2018

Today's eye evaluation with Dr. Ruggiero was full of exciting news about my vision. Dr. Teresa, as I call my Doctor, told me that all of my screening scores were tens of percentage points better than they were just six months ago. She also suggested that I write a book about Nystagmus. She noted that no one has written about it and that it would help so many people.

Her childlike joy at witnessing my successes filled me with warmth and pride. Her urging me to write a book made me want to strut around the office and shout to the world:

I have arrived!

5/25/2018 Finding Depth

Today, the long drive to Vision Therapy was stressful for no reason that I could discern. Upon arrival my eyes were shaking a bit. I was upset about this lapse, relieved when my eyes steadied after a few short exercises designed to relax the eyes. Then Dr Clay and I began exercises that would encourage my eyes to work together, to team and later fuse images so that I might develop binocular vision, and realize my dream: depth perception. We had discussed this plan and I wonder if my excitement and nerves about this created the stressful drive. For many years I have been presented with these exercises but I was not able to make any progress. I did not know that Nystagmus interferes with the ability of eyes to work in unison.

I achieved a beginner's level of binocularity almost effortlessly in the first exercise Dr Clay presented. We were both shocked, smiling, full of joy and feelings of accomplishment. Next I tried the famous "beads on a string exercise" (See the following entry on Brock String) which I have attempted for years with no success. Today my eyes worked as a team. The beginnings of binocularity evident. A hopeful step towards seeing the world with depth, just like most other humans, and the possibility of being able to walk, not trip, down stairs.

Brock String

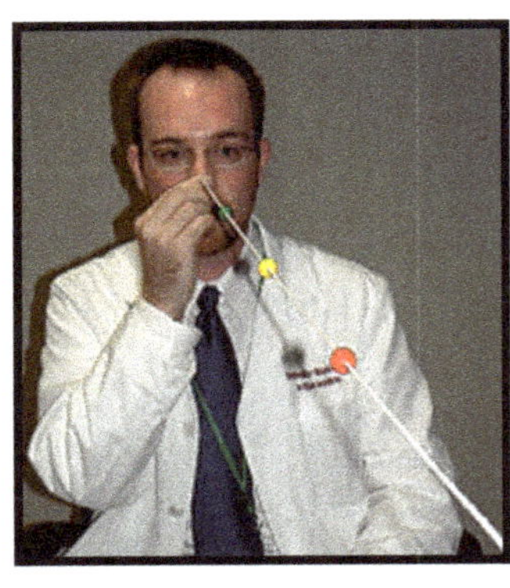

NOTE: From Wikipedia https://en.wikipedia.org/wiki/Brock_string

A Brock string (named after Frederick W. Brock) is an instrument used in vision therapy. It consists of a white string of approximately 10 feet in length with three small wooden beads of different colors.

The Brock string is commonly employed during treatment of convergence insufficiency and other anomalies of binocular vision. It is used to develop skills of convergence as well as to disrupt suppression of one of the eyes.

During therapy, the one end of the Brock string is held on the tip of the nose while the other is tied to a fixed point. The three beads are spaced out at various distances.

The patient is asked to focus on one of the beads, while noting the visual input of each eye and sensation of convergence. The patient can use variable techniques to make easier or more difficult by bringing the beads closer\further to the nose and by employing lenses and prisms.

Although this procedure is usually associated with binocular vision and anti-suppression therapy, it can also be a valuable procedure for developing accurate fixation skills under binocular conditions.

Three (to five) colored beads are spaced on a length of string at least 20 inch long. The patient is instructed to alternate fixation and focus from one bead to the next while maintaining awareness of physiological diplopia.

Set up:

1 Tie one end of the string to a doorknob. Position one bead at the end of the cord close to the doorknob. This is the far fixation bead.
2 Place the middle fixation bead about 10 inch from you.
3 Place the near fixation bead about 4 inch from you.
4 Stand directly in front of the doorknob facing it. Hold the cord up to the bridge of your nose so that the cord is stretched tight between your nose and the doorknob.

Procedure:

1 Look at the near fixation bead. Keep this bead single as you look directly at it. If the near bead is double this indicates an eye teaming problem. If this occurs move the near bead closer or further away until you see it as a single bead. The near bead should be moved closer and closer as the task becomes easier. Eventually the near bead should be only one inch from the bridge of your nose.

2. As you look at the near fixation bead you should see two strings, each of which appears to come from your eyes. If your fixation on the bead is accurate, the two strings should appear to meet exactly at the bead forming an "X". As the bead is moved to one inch from your nose, the two strings should appear to meet exactly at the bead forming a "V".
3. Shift fixation to the middle bead and then to the far bead and repeat. If your fixation of the far bead is accurate, the two strings should appear to meet exactly at the bead forming a "V".
4. Change the location of the fixation beads and again repeat.
5. Try to be aware of other objects in your field of view as you practice.
6. Slowly turn your head from side to side through an angle of about 45 degrees maintaining your vision of the two strings at all times. (if you turn too far one string will disappear)

References

Scheiman, Mitchell and Wick, Bruce. Clinical Management of Binocular Vision. Lippincott, New York. 1994. pgs 188-192. ISBN 0-7817-3275-1

5/30/2018

The past two weeks in Vision Therapy have been full of breakthroughs in mastering eye teaming exercises which have been my nemesis for the past thirty years. Now that my eyes are steady, they have been able to begin learning to work together.

My favorite exercise is with a cartoon robot. In this exercise, an image, in this case a robot, is centered within a circle on a large computer screen. The patient wears a pair of goggles equipped with electronics that move the image right or left while at the same time supporting both eyes to maintain focus. The goal is eye teaming and fusion which creates binocular vision. I had never tried this exercise before, so imagine my surprise when the robot was suddenly floating in mid air! Instead of the robot appearing only as a flat image on the screen my eyes had transitioned from monocular vision to binocular vision and voila: depth perception that allowed the robot to come off the screen. A magical leap forward on my path to finding depth.

6/13/2018 The World is Not Flat

I had no idea how flat my world has been until today.

I experienced the contrast between seeing in three dimensions, and the flat world of two dimensions within a few short hours. This experience was shattering and exciting. I achieved binocular vision in a new exercise in Vision Therapy and felt elated when I left the office.

Later that afternoon lying on my sun porch daybed, as I looked at the bedpost and wrought iron like frame I realized that I was seeing a cardboard cutout pasted onto the wall behind it. Black painted on a burnt orange wall. I knew that it wasn't painted or pasted on a wall, that it had its own space, a solid object in front of a wall.

But it looked pasted on and as I gazed around the room I saw a room full of furniture pasted onto the log frame walls of the sun porch.

I began to slowly absorb how I have always seen the world. I felt horrified, physically ill. As I write, I look out the window by my writing place at the azaleas and woodlands all around. It is beautiful and it is flat. The pain of this awakening carries despair. I see hope on the path I am walking with my Vision Therapy guides.

Aside: *For those with binocular vision, the concept of monocular vision is hard to conceive. Try this experiment. Hold this book a distance away from your eyes. Hold your thumb up between your face and the book. Now, close one eye. While you know that your thumb is a distance away from the book, your thumb appears to be on the same plane as the book. It may be more clear or larger. Your mind is filling in details because you are used to seeing things in 3D, so your mind is interpreting the 2D it is seeing and translating on the fly.*

Now open both eyes. You can see the space between thumb and page.

Close one eye again.

You will see the difference between two dimensions and three dimensions.

7/15/2018

I wonder why I have abandoned writing for a month. The monumental change in my vision has transformed my life and yet I act like it's nothing. So untrue. I am living my own miracle.

Yesterday a short encounter with Deb, an old friend and coworker, refocused my attention on my amazing new improved sight. We have known each other for over twenty years. She noted that I looked different and went on to explain that I used to tilt my head and squint when I spoke to her and now I look straight at her face into her eyes. This hard won connection so worth the effort restored my faith and drove me back to the keys.

7/17/2018

I want to tell my story, but sometimes I feel distant from it. When I return to the keyboard, I reconnect. The encounter with my friend Deb was significant. I remember always tilting my head, I saw that pose so often in the mirror. I was not aware of the squinting she mentioned. My friend seeing the absence of these behaviors was another little victory.

I wonder how much of my sadness as a child grew from feeling separate and far away from people whose facial expressions I could not read. I lacked the intimacy of eye contact, a deficit with far reaching effects. I knew the moment I tried to look directly at someone's face the uncomfortable feeling in my eyes would start. Suddenly my eyes would feel frozen in their sockets and I could no longer see clearly. I would struggle to see, but I was not able to control my eyes. The experience was more frightening because I never understood why my eyes stopped working. I avoided looking at the faces of people, worried I looked freakish. I am more aware of the loneliness and isolation I experienced. I had friends but I was so distant... I lived life this way until four months ago.

7/20/2018

Meditation group last night brought out once again the new way I meet my life. I sat in the room with eight other people and spoke to them as a different person than I was just two months ago when last we sat together. I am calm, solid, bigger. I fill up the space around me. I do not hide, nor am I timid or apologetic. I speak my story in a clear loud voice, looking around at everyone, proud of myself and who I have become. Sad again as I write, for the years of loss of self. The misery I lived had so much to do with my frozen visual world, the blur, the distance, the denial that my world was different and I was not dull or crazy.

7/24/2018

I spent all of my life navigating a world that could freeze at any moment. I used to look at something .a person's face, a sun dappled road, and the image would freeze right before my eyes. I would try to focus, try to clear my vision, move my eyes, and they simply would not move. They remained fixed no matter what I did. I would breathe, try to relax, pull off the road if I was driving. If talking to someone, I would look away, breathe, try to get a grip on my very frightened self.

I do not know if anyone understood what I experienced. The eye doctors I have seen over many years listed Nystagmus as one of my eye disorders, but they didn't talk to me about how the rapid movement of my eyes affected my sight. I didn't even understand my experience completely until the Nystagmus was gone. I knew that my eyes would suddenly feel stuck, that I couldn't see whatever I was trying to focus on. Occasionally a friend would tell me my eyes were moving real fast, but I could not see this in the mirror as hard as I tried to catch the rapid movement.

Now my eyes move freely, focusing on the object of my attention. I am in charge of my eyes instead of my vision being shut down by the Nystagmus. My eyes no longer freeze. They do not get stuck. I am not suddenly blinded by dappling sunlight on a country road. I am able to see, my world feels wide open, expansive.

Driving

In the past I usually felt that my eyes weren't open all the way like they are now. Everything looked flat. Colors were dull. Nothing drew my attention. I concentrated on maneuvering my car in and out of traffic, avoiding obstacles, not really looking at my environment. Nothing seemed very concrete. It was like I was in a hazy fog. I didn't try to see any particular thing I passed, just kept my car on the road. Stayed between the lines, focusing on nothing else but those lines and the other cars. I couldn't find destinations, because I didn't dare to look for them, because I knew I couldn't take my eyes off the road for an instant. I know now that my nervousness while driving kept the Nystagmus active most of the time I was in the car. A frightening thought. A terrifying experience that I never understood until it was over.

9/16/2018 School Daze

I grew up not knowing I had a visual disability, that I was living a totally different life than my peers. I had a couple good girlfriends from my neighborhood with whom I spent most of my out-of-school hours.

School was a scary place where I felt alone because I could not see well enough to find my friends in the crowd of kids at lunch or recess.

I remember always feeling afraid because I couldn't find friends to sit with in the cafeteria. I didn't want to walk over to lunch tables full of kids only to feel lost staring at unfamiliar faces. I acted like I was fine standing awkwardly with my tray before finding a place to sit alone at a table.

My only memory of being on the playground was once taking a bad spill down a concrete ramp and getting a bloody skinned knee. I have no recollection of playing with other kids.

I only saw things that were very close to me. Everything more than a few feet from me almost didn't exist. I also had to touch things to know they were really what I thought they were. I didn't trust my sight. This has always been true and still is the case in many situations.

Wherever I walk, it is always best if I can slide my feet,

feeling everything beneath, instead of lifting my feet and having the uncertain feeling that when I put my foot down, the ground may not be where I thought it was.

I also had the fear of bumping into things as this happened quite often. I used to hit my head on walls and furniture. I recall slamming my head into a concrete building. Glass doors were a hazard. Sometimes the impact was hard enough to cause a woozy feeling.

9/18/2018 Miracle

I am told by people who have witnessed my journey into sight, that I have achieved a miracle. I am shown awe and respect, described as a strong, determined and disciplined individual. I am blind to these accolades. I grew up believing I was stupid, clumsy and socially inept. I thought I lacked coordination because I could not catch a ball. I thought I was dumb because I could not decipher the writing on the blackboard. I lived on the fringes of my peer group, too afraid to engage.

Nobody told me that I was legally blind, that I had a disability which impaired my abilities in many far reaching areas of development. I lived my life blind to the impact of my disability until I met Dr Ruggiero who was the first person who explained to me how much I had overcome with my limited sight. I will never forget the day she told me that my sight was so poor, I processed information I read at a first grade reading level. Despite this, I had earned two master's degrees with these limited reading skills. That evening in a conversation with my sister whose intellect I idolize, I cried as she helped me see the brilliance I possessed to have gotten so far academically.

I wonder what my life would have been like if I had known that I lived with a debilitating challenge that made so many things harder for me. I wonder if I would have appreciated my successes. I wonder if I would have walked through life with self assurance. I wonder if I would now honor the miracle I am living. It is not too late. I am living proof.

10/10/2018 Going Public

I have been guarded about talking about my vision, only sharing my story with people I trust. Today I went public. My friend teaches nursing students a class in Cultural Competency. She invited me to be a guest speaker to talk about how my "disability" has impacted my life in order to help nurses better understand the culture of disabled people. I have never been called a person with a disability -- a truth finally told. I stood up in front of a pool of glazed over eyes set in bored faces. I watched their faces wake up as I told my story. They listened as I shared how my terrible vision affected my life, how I coped and how I overcame this "disability". Their rapt attention and soul searching questions proved that they understood and respected my long journey.

A student asked "Why do you think your parents didn't tell you about your disability?" I have asked myself this question for thirty years. I paused as I felt again the sadness of my parents' silence, the agony of not having invaluable information that would have changed the trajectory of my life. In one simple question, this young woman validated my experience of the lost opportunity of my parent's silence. She also normalized their silence as we spoke about their possible reasons for keeping my blindness secret. Perhaps it was not neglect but rather their desire to protect, combined with ignorance and insecurity about how to deal with this frightening, overwhelming burden.

10/18/2018 Post MST

I have treated my vision journey as commonplace. I have minimized the effort I exerted to survive, overcome, and thrive. I have never "seen" the person who looks back at me in the mirror: a spirit who wanted something unattainable and made it happen. I have achieved so much in this one "small" accomplishment which has been a huge, earth shattering feat. My doctor is amazed. Friends and family who see the changes look at me in awe.

The way I move through my life has been dramatically altered. I used to tilt my head to one side, unable to meet people directly, look a person in the eye. I was always afraid when driving, not knowing when my eyes would lose focus. I didn't bother to look at the landscape I drove by and now I look around, marveling at the countryside. It has taken nine months for me to fully appreciate the changes, another birth along my journey into sight.

10/28/2018 Balanced

I had another "small" vision breakthrough today during a silent meditation retreat. The class was invited to do a standing yoga practice which involved two balance poses requiring a person to stand on one foot.

I have never been able to do these balance postures but today was different. I felt more solid standing on one foot, less wobbly in the poses. I realized that the eye teaming, binocularity exercises in Vision Therapy had improved my balance.

Monocular vision impedes balance because the eyes are seeing two separate targets instead of one focal point. A singular point of focus which is achieved with binocular vision is needed to support the body's ability to balance. I have attempted these balance poses unsuccessfully for 40 years. I triumphed today.

11/3/2018 Teamwork

Eye teaming is a step in the process of developing binocular vision. I am sixty-seven years old and my eyes have never worked together. My right eye turns in, which causes my eyes to see different views of everything upon which they focus. Without the ability to focus as a team my eyes are incapable of fusing images together. Fusion creates binocular vision which results in depth perception, something which has been absent from my vision.

Vision Therapy exercises that teach eyes to team demand that the brain develops this skill. As a sixty-seven year old student, these five minute exercises leave me dizzy and completely exhausted. Knowing that I am trying to rewire my brain is both exciting and hard to comprehend. Each week the exercises increase in difficulty and I am amazed as I master each skill, ready to move on to a more challenging exercise.

11/26/2018 Mirage

A few weeks ago, as I strolled into town with the little dog one evening, I noticed lights in the distance. As we drew closer, I learned that these lights lined the streets - buildings rising beside them, dimly lit in the early dusk. Soon I saw a little town and suddenly I realized that I was seeing my sleepy little town in the distance, just over the bridge.

I have walked this path countless times in my fifteen years here and have never seen the town that lay up ahead. I only walked in my bubble of frozen semi-permeable walls.

Trying to push through walls which enclosed my sight proved ineffective. My efforts never ceased. As useless and painful as my attempts were, I felt there had to be a way through the barrier which limited my sight, my connection with the outside world. I was frightened within the walls, always straining to see through them. Sheer joy in my newfound freedom. Pain sorely remembered.

12/11/2018 What Happens When a Person Sees Too Much

The world got too big for me today and I was scared. A simple drive to a town forty-five minutes from me for my annual Christmas shopping shook me up, woke me up, and made me face a brand new realization about my sight.

Things around me don't look the same anymore and that can be quite disorienting, which in a car, can be unsettling, and a bit dangerous if I were being completely honest.

I was driving along a route I have driven for thirty years and suddenly on my right there was a huge building that had never been there before. This building took up a city block. I saw another addition to the city scape across the street adding to my discomfort. And then a car came out of nowhere far enough ahead for me to have time to react, but still a slightly unnerving experience to have been so distracted.

The worst part, however, was quickly acknowledging that the city scape actually was unchanged. The Firehouse had stood there years before my time. I am the change agent here. I have never seen the Fire Station, the heart of the town, until today.

It is difficult to understand why the gift of seeing a larger world can be so frightening. Perhaps it is the loss of the familiar, the lack of control, the awareness that anything might pop out at me from nowhere, completely unexpected.

12/14/2018 Small Spaces

I am a small person and always thought that my diminutive stature was the source of my comfort in small spaces. Now I question that reasoning.

I feel safe in a smaller world, one that I can hold close, near enough to touch, search out the shape of images with my fingers. I know the world through a kind of 3D braille of my senses. I see and know things that are physically within my reach.

I used to listen for oncoming traffic to cross streets, trusting my other senses more than my eyes. Eyes that so often failed me leaving me confused and embarrassed. As my eyes have improved I notice that I "look both ways" more often than listen for oncoming cars.

I am secure and confident in what I know about my surroundings when they are within my grasp. I am not much of an explorer of things far away.

I look closely and deep into the world. As an adult I have often crawled along a pavement to view the tiny creatures found there, as a child would do. I have gotten down on all fours in grass to see, smell and touch the first bluets in the Spring.

I want life as close to me as I can get to her. When something is far from me and I want to know it better, I move in close.

Up until this year, when I could not gain access to the "object of my desire", my mind and senses would shut down. I became numb, and feigned a nonchalant disinterest. This lack of interest was a lie. I felt so alone and isolated at those times when I longed to see and experience something and had to let it go, give up.

12/23/2018 Seeing Sparkle

It's Christmas time and I've chosen to give my 8 year old great nephew Henry a treasure from my small collection of crystals. I have a raw piece of amethyst just the right size for a small boy's hand.

I was given this piece over thirty years ago by a close friend who has passed. It is precious for its sentimental value, unremarkable in color or shine. I have often tried and failed to appreciate its natural beauty.

I cleaned it prior to boxing it up for Henry and then I looked at it, one last time. To my surprise I saw the sparkle of deep purple diamonds, brilliant points of light, revealed by the touch of soft gray sunlight. A piece of purple earth now beautiful to my eyes that see.

1/1/2019 The Yoga Teacher

I met Sandy, a yoga teacher, on the final day of 2018. We met for our "class" in her beautifully decorated, but very small apartment. I was sent to her by my doc in the hope that she could help me gain flexibility, possibly an antidote to the leaden feeling in my body.

I have practiced Yoga on and off since my thirties, striving to look and feel like the toned and limber Yoga acrobats around me. Yoga was something to conquer. I never achieved the relaxation and enjoyment that I felt was expected. I stretched past my limits forcing my breath into my wrenched muscles. Relief came at the end of class, the twenty minute guided relaxation when we were allowed to flop on the mat and "nap."

This yoga teacher, Sandy, invited me to move any way my body felt like moving! She did not instruct me to move into yoga postures. Her only guidance was to take care not to inflict pain on myself to achieve the most stretch, a revolutionary idea.

She suggested that I move like a bird! She guided me to move my fingers, feeling them as they moved. This quirky woman, five years my senior, asked me to move with the innocence of a child, the way babies explore their newfound world. I practiced being curious, feeling every small movement in my body.

I cried many times in our Yoga "class" and shared with

Sandy how this kind, gentle approach was a welcome contrast to how my body has been treated throughout my entire life. She reached a place inside me that no other person had ever touched. This one meeting with Sandy allowed me to begin to heal my damaged relationship to my body. Since then I have been able to disconnect trauma experiences from the living breathing body I inhabit. An incredible gift.

1/2/2019 Frozen Numb

My eyes often felt frozen. My body has felt numb probably 75% of the time for as long as I can remember. I see a connection here. I am unable to respond when asked how my body feels. I am all mind and emotion.

I love to swim and dance. I feel the water, the music, but not the instrument that moves me fluidly with these forces. I feel the texture and weight of the plants and earth as I garden. I am super strong despite my small stature. I am aware of tired, aching muscles, but I push my body past its tolerance as I am unaware of my breaking point.

I do not fully experience this living, breathing body. I have felt for so long that my eyes were empty orbs frozen, sealed shut, ignoring everything, trying not to see. I have felt blind and numb. I wonder if my body experience has in part arisen from my frozen eyes that left me feeling sealed in, cut off, shut down. I had little feeling in my body, minimal awareness. I felt closed off from the outside world where I did not feel safe.

1/3/2019 Anxiety in the Legally Blind Person

I have been a worry wart as long as I can remember. Anxiety is a huge "force to be reckoned with" in my life. I have never associated anxiety with my limited sight.

My vision difficulties were not spoken about in my family, a choice made with good intentions I believe. I stumbled, fumbled, averted my eyes, dared not to make eye contact, pretended not to look too hard at things, so as not to appear stupid and inept.

I could not recognize familiar people, even when they were in my face. I could not read street signs, bulletin boards, movie marquees, menus posted in delis.

A mailbox might appear to be a person. Yet it never occurred to me that my anxious nature came from this hidden environment that was my world. The depth of this awareness is astounding.

Random Entry

I am a small person in constant motion, a "whirling dervish" comes to mind.

I am practicing the art of slow movement. Benefits are many. I no longer crash into stationary objects, now able to navigate around things as I have learned to take the time to stop.

Random Entry

Color is another difficulty.

Black people often look the same to me, but so do whites! I have had African American siblings as patients and gotten them confused - unforgivable shame.

Pretty blonde Caucasian girls also look the same. White mistakes bring embarrassment. Black errors - shame. Evidence of unseen prejudice.

Imagine running into friends, clients, neighbors and having no idea if they are who you think they might be? Or total strangers? Shame.

January, 2019 Mirror, Mirror

Little girls, pre-pubescents, teens, young women maturing into older women, crones ... women learn throughout our lives to gaze at our reflection in the mirror, to dream, and to wonder who we will become, how we will be seen by others. Do we like the image that appears before us or hold the image in disdain?

Hours upon hours are spent on this life long exercise of knowing our feminine image. Searching, looking into our eyes, observing the changes in our face, the strongest, most immediate "calling card" when we meet another human: face to face. The power of the face. We don't say body to body, it is our face that tells our story, reveals our fear, sadness, anger and love, all seen in our facial expressions.

Today a mirror was hung over my bathroom sink in which I can see my face for the first time in my life. Not just pieces of it as I teeter on tip toe. I can stand flat footed on the bathroom tile and simply look into my eyes, admire my green and purple hair. I can see the shine of delicate-rose-petal-pink-skin, damp from a steamy tub of lavender bubbles. I can soak in this intimacy, free from the eyes and opinions of onlookers. The mirror is a huge oval and although not much of it is filled with my image I feel the enormity of myself in this looking glass. I wonder how seeing myself in this way will change how I meet my life.

1/23/2019 Go Fetch

Simple game of fetch played with the little dog since she was a pup. I have never been able to throw sticks too far. They always ended up falling to the ground too near to warrant a chase by my four legged friend.

I thought I just had a poor throwing arm. This Winter on a non-extraordinary walk in the woods with her, I could see that when I threw a stick it would get caught up in the trees.

When I looked closer, I could see paths through the trees that I had never seen. I realized I could aim my sticks through the spaces BETWEEN the trees, and the sticks would fly forever, followed by my happy little dog.

Over and over, we played with the flying sticks. I remembered all my big, kind hearted dogs who would run the two feet my sticks used to go, retrieving sticks wagging tails, tongues hanging out of big drooling smiles, patient, accepting my limitations with puppy love.

1/28/2019 Blind to What Was Kept Silent

Spending my childhood legally blind is a metaphor for my life that only now I am beginning to see. My limited vision was kept secret, I believe, in hopes of shielding me from feeling that I was different from my peers.

Without this knowledge, however, I grew to see myself in a false light. I saw myself as a person who functioned poorly in many areas. I felt bad about myself because there were so many things I could not do. I did not know that my sight was damaged, not my entire self.

I did not know that my difficulty navigating life was due to my severely limited sight and not due to a deep systemic deformity.

I spent a lot of time by myself in my closet playing with tiny figurines, creating a pretend world of friends and family. I felt safe in this small space away from the prying eyes and ears of my parents who worried and fretted about me, trying to keep me safe but not giving me enough space to explore and find my own way.

I shut down my emotions to safe guard my inner self, mirroring the way my eyes were closed to seeing the world around me. This combination left me feeling very much alone.

2/2/2019

Sometimes I am complacent about my newfound sight. I stop noticing the breathtaking experience of seeing clearly. I forget to search and look carefully at everything around me. Then I become afraid that the clarity has vanished in the night while I lay sleeping, or was merely an illusion, something I wished for so hard that I convinced myself it was real. Self -fulfilling prophecy, a wake up call to pay attention. I need to fight the old habit of not looking that evolved from a life of not seeing.

I spent my life only seeing things close to me clearly enough to make them interesting. The world beyond five feet was a soft collage of people and objects I identified by sound, color, and shape. I excelled at deductive reasoning. I pretended that I could see the same world as other people so as not to draw attention to myself. The silence about my limitations taught me to keep quiet about my struggle to see. I don't recall asking people to identify themselves when they were out of my range of sight, and definitely did not think to ask a friend if the mailbox we were passing was really a person I knew.

2/2019 White Lie Revealed

People have been shocked when they catch a glimpse of the severity of my visual impairment. At those moments I felt like a freak and pretended my visual error was accidental, that I was not in the dark at all. I became a skilled impostor and kept my secret hidden.

It is curious that I never asked my parents why I could not see like other kids. I did not acknowledge my difference. I was blind to my blindness. My parents wanted me to feel normal, that I was just like everyone else. I assimilated that big white lie.

My first experience of sharing the truth about my vision with another person occurred when I was a preteen. I was walking home from school with my best friend Shelly when I looked at something white ahead of us and named the object, inaccurately of course. Shelly nonchalantly told me the true identity of the object. In that moment our friendship grew deeper as I realized that although I had asked about an object that did not exist, Shelly knew exactly of what I was speaking. The best gift ever, she understood my visual world. Up until that moment I had been completely alone. My first glimmer of hope that another person could enter my confusing world.

When other rare friends throughout my life have shared the depth of Shelly's insight I have felt closer, happy that another person has seen the world through my eyes.

2/8/2019 In Depth - Day of Days !!!

When I was born, my right eye turned inward while my left eye looked straight ahead. When I was five and again at age fifteen I underwent surgeries on my right eye to align the malingering eye with my obedient left eye. I was told that the surgeries were primarily cosmetic and of little consequence to my visual abilities.

I have monocular vision, an uncommon condition. Most people are born with binocular vision. Binocular vision allows the right and left eye to focus on the same thing, fuse it, and form a three dimensional image in the brain.

People with monocular vision are not able to direct their eyes to look precisely at the same thing. They see two slightly different images that cannot be formed into a single picture. The result is that people with Monocular vision see in two dimensions instead of three. The world of a person with Monocular vision is flat.

I have known for thirty-five years that I have monocular vision and have been striving to develop binocular vision. I did not know until a year ago that my misaligned right eye was the direct cause of this problem.

I also did not fully understand the severity of my

lack of depth perception.

I had none, I still have none.

This week, during my three month eye evaluation, for a half hour I experienced binocular or stereoscopic vision!

With the help of a trial pair of prism lenses, I saw the world in three dimensions, with depth, for the first time.

I cried tears of joy, and grief over what I have missed.

2/15/2019 Brave New World

I am used to a world of soft color, line and texture. I feel safe there.

I do not know if I can adapt to a bold new world of sharp angles, deep edges, vibrant color.

I feel as if the world is jumping out in front of me at every turn. There is nowhere to hide, to rest. No escape from seeing everything. I wonder if I feel I am more seen, and so, am more vulnerable. I am excited and scared. I have spent my life in a world of haze and shadow.

A totally blind person knows their way around their dark world. In my world of limited sight I have lived comfortably within the landscape I have known.

I am not sure if I can learn to navigate a whole new world and feel safe.

2/17/2019 A Shift in Dimensions

Soon I will see the world in three dimensions instead of two. My world will no longer appear hollow, flat, indistinct, lifeless.

I am habituated to seeing the world this way. It is only now, since I have experienced a different reality, that I am beginning to look with eyes wide open and see the flat-lander experience I have lived. "I never knew what I was missing" barely describes my shock and disbelief when I compare this world to the one I glimpsed two weeks ago.

I feel sad, floating in salty tears as I attempt to integrate what it has meant to live without depth perception. I believed I stumbled down stairs out of clumsiness, not that I was unable to see where to step. I thought that I jumped curbs and traffic islands while driving out of stupidity, not the inability to determine depth.

Since my glimpse of a world with depth, now thrown back into a two dimensional world, nothing looks "right".

I feel like I am living in a movie set. Suddenly it looks as if the beams and logs that hold my house together lack substance, appear to be pasted on the walls. I want to tear up this cardboard mock up and build a real three dimensional world, from scratch.

2/18/2019 False Sight

This morning, the little dog and I walked along the river at the bottom of our hill. A light fluffy snow frosted the brown slush left over from last week's snow, meager offerings this year to these two intrepid snow lovers. It takes only a bit of new fallen snow to inspire the little dog to run with leaps and bounds and burrow head first though the white fluff, full of puppy joy. I watch and laugh at her antics as I hum Christmas carols. I notice the quaint New England homes dotting the roads of my tiny hill town and realize with sadness that the images I see are simply picture postcards -- flat, painted in two dimensions against the slate gray sky.

The scene I see is not real, just color put to canvas and nothing more. I feel the distance between myself and my surroundings profoundly now and wonder how much the flatness of my world view has defined my relationship to all the places I have inhabited. Has this fueled my sense of isolation, fed my anxiety? I feel and see things if I roll around in them like the little dog, but I don't feel engaged when just my eyes are the source of information. My eyes do not guide me well . They allow me to slam into doors and walls. My eyes do not keep me free from harm. Instead they betray me. I am sad knowing that I can not rely on myself. The fact that I look perfectly "normal" adds to my challenge. I do not look blind, nor do I appear to have a visual disability. I just appear clumsy, awkward, incompetent and foolish, not appealing attributes to wear while walking through life.

2/21/2019 Seeing Loss

Most evenings now, I gaze around my log home and feel bereft. The walls feel hollow, without substance or weight. They do not have the stature of the buildings I saw through the prism lenses, the world of three dimensions. All the beautiful and cozy furnishings, I find lacking.

I know it is my new awareness of actually "SEEING" what I have always seen that is causing this painful loss, this empty feeling. But I feel a need to experience the truth of what has always been, to grieve it, to appreciate myself for how I navigated this solitary place for so long.

2/23/2019 Distortion

This morning as the little dog and I walked down our country lane, I noticed the evergreens darkening the hill in the distance. The leash grew taut so I turned to look back at my four legged companion and found her with paws planted eyes fixed on me, clearly demanding that we were to go no further. I explained to her that our path was just icy and gave a gentle tug. We moved onward very slowly, only a few paces. Then I saw that the evergreen up on the hill was not really above us in the distance, but instead was an ancient branch that had blown off a large spruce tree and was blocking the driveway.

Each time now when I am confronted with my lack of depth perception I am shocked. I am living in between two contrasting and conflicting worlds, I find myself in a constant state of awe and wonder. I am struck by what I have been living with for so long, navigating my distorted surroundings with just my wits and ability to adapt. My joyful anticipation of the new world I shall enter any day now is glorious.

2/24/2019 No Longer Stupid

Driving a car has been nerve wracking for me, since I got my license 30 years ago. Up until two weeks ago, I thought that certain dangerous errors I made were due to ignorance, stupidity.

I have a tendency to jump curbs, not such a big deal. A few times however I have made potentially dangerous mistakes.

At intersections where I need to make a left turn and there is a median strip, the median just looks like a brick and cement part of the flat road. I cannot tell if it is a raised median or a decorative crossing. I often cannot see far enough to see the street or lot I want to turn into.

Because I can't tell if the median is raised or only a change in color or material, I am unable to determine whether to turn in front of it or on the far side to make my turn.

So I guess.

Sometimes I guess wrong. I have turned in front of median strips, ending up facing oncoming traffic. I keep to low traffic roads so it has been easy to make a quick maneuver back to safety. The fear and shame has not been so easy to leave behind. These near misses have been over in an instant, never enough time for me to analyze and learn from my mistake. Yesterday I finally understood the error of my ways and how to make a correction.

I was driving home with the little dog from her favorite

place, the local pet food store, with its adoring, treat-giving clerks, doggie clientele, and the much needed new toy at the end of each trip, when another accident was avoided. This time was different from the others. There was the upcoming left hand turn, the median strip, my nerves about to fray, but I watched and waited as a car crossed in front of me, going onto the road I was seeking, keeping the median strip between our vehicles.

I could not see the road that went on the opposite side of the strip, but I could see where the other car was going, so I knew where to steer my car. Observing where this car was going allowed me to easily make the turn just by following the path of the other car. I went merrily on my way home not having to deal with the honk of horns, or the terror of facing oncoming traffic. I also came to a shocking realization. I have been driving in a flat world for almost thirty years, and I never understood my disadvantage.

I wonder if my lack of depth perception had been explained to me along with ways to adapt, if I would have felt safer. I have similar questions about driving with Nystagmus, the condition that caused my eyes to constantly shake.

It was terrifying to have my vision freeze, to lose the ability to focus. I was not taught how to manage this debilitating situation. The combination of these two conditions and serious nearsightedness made driving very difficult.

I believed I was just an incompetent driver. I believed I was scared in the car because I was an anxious person. I did not know that my struggles driving were due to the fact that I was not driving on an equal playing field.

3/1/2019 Safe Travels

I will head out today on a long drive to catch the train in Hudson, NY to travel to Philadelphia to see my family. Scary memories of making this drive make for an anxious morning. I know I will immediately become happy and relaxed as soon as I arrive "home"and the trip is behind me. The knot in my stomach this morning comes from the nagging anxiety of a lengthy drive on fast roads, scarier than the slow windy drive on the mountain road I travel into town each week. Today's Winter sun shining on white snow and the dull brown gray landscape will impede my ability to interpret my surroundings and see what lies ahead. I navigate roadways more easily in Spring, Summer, and Fall when the multi-hued landscape adds valuable visual cues that help me see the borders of the road more clearly and avoid obstacles more easily identified.

As I wait for my special prism lenses which will grant entrance into a world of depth, I picture how driving with depth perception will differ from driving in the "flatlands." Basking in the winter light on my sun porch, perched over my laptop I feel the joy of possibility. I imagine what it will be like to see the rise of a curb or the depth of a ditch along a shoulder, signs that tell a driver NOT to pull over and take a break, that these spots are not safe havens, as they often appear to me. I pause here, stunned remembering years of terror on the road.

3/2/2019 White Cane

Yesterday I found myself waiting for a train in an unfamiliar station. Seeking assurance that I would catch my train and not head to an unplanned destination, I sought the advice of fellow travelers as to where and how to hop on the correct railway car. I shared with each traveler that I do not see very well as an explanation for my need for assistance. People were either knowledgeable or not, each trying to help. One woman made quite an impression.

She approached me and offered the unsolicited advice that procuring a white cane might be helpful. After a stunned pause I told her firmly yet politely that my vision was not so bad that I needed a blind man's cane! (I left out the descriptor.)

She was not put off and continued with purpose, sharing that she was a nurse and knew that a white cane would alert people that I was in need of help navigating my surroundings. Yet again I fended off her advances, only after her third attempt did I succeed in putting a stop to her mission. Grateful, I watched her retreat defeated, leaving me free once again to enjoy an opportunity to observe my life as a visually impaired person incognito.

Later, as I settled into the train ride to visit my family I had the startling realization that a white cane would have helped in my life of stumbling over curbs, steps, sidewalks, hiking trails, all hazardous for a person who lacks depth perception.

I was never told that I lacked depth perception. I never understood why I sometimes fell down stairs or tripped on a stone walkway. I was always surprised.

It only occurred to me over many years of falling down that I should slide my feet along uneven ground as I do now.

Sadness washes over me, then I smile. A new world is coming my way soon.

3/19/201 Prism Lenses! New Sight

The prism lenses arrived last week.

I went to Northampton and Dr. Ruggiero put them on. I didn't trust myself to drive with the new lenses yet. My friend drove me home. Now, I still feel as if I have woken up in a brand new world. Nothing looks the same as it did before the precious lenses were placed upon my face. I remember looking around the office, seeing the staff, everyone and everything clear, bright, popping out at me, separate from the background. In addition to providing some depth perception the new lenses have added a clarity I have never experienced. This is a huge added benefit unexpected by Dr. Ruggiero, and me.

I had no idea that I was living in a blurry world until now. It was all I knew. I am able to see faces clearly now. Complexions, wrinkles, tears of joy in the caring eyes of my Vision Therapy family, as they share my happiness. My experience of the world has exploded. I am often in shock, in a daze, trying to absorb the changes. Stepping outside I am awed by rooftops that stand separate from the blue sky, mundane architecture turned magnificent, a feast for my new eyes.

Driving has revealed perhaps the most stunning vision show. Rivers, rock faces lining the roads, hills in the distance, now pop out, distinct. No longer do I see a painted landscape. Cars have become alive, bright, vivid, moving metal creatures that bear no likeness to the dull vehicles of a week ago. I am even drawn to peer into cars to see the human behind the wheel, something I never attempted. Cars appeared driverless before now - just blurs behind the wheel.

I am overwhelmed by all that I am seeing. It is too much to absorb. I need to slow down, take in each new sight. I am riding waves of an experience that begs to be taken moment by moment, savored, contemplated. I am driven to put on the brakes. Stop time, cease to do anything else in my life except look, see, search the world around me. I long to investigate all the hidden crevices so as not to miss a single thing ever again. I want to see everything. My entire life has changed in an instant. Too much too fast for my brain to understand, to integrate.

With regret I notice that at times I am missing so much as I slip back into my well-worn habit of not looking, honed over decades of giving up the futile effort to see what could not be seen. My eyes are finally strong, steady, clear, focused and I intend to give them free reign to guide me to all the places that are no longer out of sight.

3/19/2019

Now, whenever I am aware of using my eyes, I become quickly overwhelmed with all that I am seeing. I need to slow down and take in each new sight. I feel like I am coasting through an experience that begs to be taken moment by moment, savored, contemplated. I want to stop time. Cease to do anything else in my life except look and see and search the world around me for more, to dig deep into all the hidden crevices so as not to miss a single thing ever again.

I want to see everything. My entire life has changed in an instant, too much, too fast for my brain to know, to integrate.

I am missing so much as I slip into my daily habit of not looking, honed over so many decades of giving up, ignoring the world around me. Lost, wandering, striving to find my way without the basic tools of sight.

I can't let go of the nagging feeling that comes with the awareness that I am not seeing everything of which I am now capable. I know that I gloss over, rush past so many opportunities to see more depth and detail, and I need to understand this tendency. It is perhaps an automatic, natural, shutting down to protect myself from overloading my system while it adapts to this new wealth of information. I am somewhat disturbed when I notice that I am allowing my gorgeous new world to drift by unnoticed.

3/20/2019

I do not know how to live this miracle everyday ... how to take in magic every time I really look at something. Nothing is even remotely the same as it was just a week ago. When I am driving, I really see the cars coming towards me, instead of often being surprised as cars would emerge as if from a fog of nothingness. They are sharp-edged, shining machines with people driving them. I am beginning to look at people, as I know there is a possibility now that I might identify drivers as neighbors and friends. I have lived so long in this fog.

Spring arrived today and with it came a new awareness of light in my kitchen. I have wood floors that were stripped and polished this fall. They shone today with a light and color I had not seen before. My kitchen felt like a brand new place full of light, open and welcoming.

In the woods today, I saw so many trees for the very first time, trees I have walked by for many years and never seen. I saw trees that fell down this past winter and felt the impact of these great living things lying now on my woodland floor, like giants taken down by a huge force in an unseen battle under cover of white snow and shrill screaming wind. Perhaps ice brought them down, I never felt their weight before now, due to the soft blur in which I moved.

4/9/2019 Emerging From the Blur/Fog

Prism lenses have provided an unexpected benefit besides depth perception. I see with a clarity that I have never known and it is quite a shock. The combination of this clarity and some depth perception is changing my life experience.

The world is now constructed of bright, crisp sharp edges, vibrant with color, richly textured, not the bland soft images I have known. I feel drawn into the trees, hills, streams, the country road on which I live. I sink into the world around me. Every single day I choose to open my eyes and look around. The change in my vision gives me an emotional and mental clarity -- sharp, imbued with enhanced purpose and direction.

I was not aware that I was living in a blurry world until my world became clear.

When people wanted to know if my vision was blurry, I reassured them that this was not an issue. I saw clearly, I was just severely near-sighted. I did not know I was living in a blurry world until I put on the prism lenses.

I often felt like an outsider. I assumed this was caused by unfounded insecurity, worry, fear -- a personal flaw or weakness. I am beginning to see that I had plenty to be afraid of, but of this I was not aware. I thought I saw the world everyone else saw. I didn't know that I had limited tools with which to interpret the world. I see now that this created a great amount of anxiety. My brother recalls my tentativeness when reaching for something. I never could see what I was trying to grasp.

I was a legally blind person who appeared to have sight.

I looked like a normal person, but one who was usually nervously treading lightly on the perimeter of life, never trusting that I knew where I was going, always trying to appear like I was sure of myself, never asking anyone for help, because I thought I had all the tools that my fellow humans possessed.

And I did not. Not even close.

4/22/2019 Fear

I am afraid even when there is nothing to fear. It has been my default setting my entire life, beginning in childhood, continuing into my sixty-eighth year. Fear haunts me daily, even when life is good and all is right in my world. Fear lurks in the shadows, creeps up on me unaware. Fear arises as I reveal it here. I dislike the words, phrases describing my fear, tossed together like a garbage salad. I show myself little care and compassion when I am afraid, loathing the experience. Hating, blaming myself for this wretched flaw.

I believe now that limited sight has been a primary source of fear. This knowledge softens my harsh self judgment. Not being able to see where I was headed or what was coming at me would feel scary, dangerous, unsafe. A troubled family life did not ease my anxiety, and my Mom, bless and rest her soul, worried and fretted most of her life, teaching me some ineffective coping skills. Genetics also play a huge part in developing anxiety.

Writing eases the morning fear, reminding me of the wisdom of my mentor Gail, who encourages me to welcome each mood or feeling as it arises with kindness and curiosity, instead of beating it into submission or some other "easier" feeling, as I am prone to do. Soaking in the warmth of this early Spring day, tapping the keys has improved my mood as well. Glorious.

4/23/2019 Fear Rears Its Ugly Head Again

Since I began wearing my remarkable prism lenses, opening an amazing new world of sight, I have not been visited by anxiety each morning. I am relieved, grateful. The past week of attacks to my professional integrity by an angry abusive father of one of my small therapy clients has cut a hole in my spirit that has allowed fear to sneak back in. The old queasiness in my gut has found its way back into my mornings and I don't like it one bit. "Embrace every moment." I hear in my head along with the old familiar chatter of an anxious mind. I take slow deep breaths, which brings a smile, a new beginning, lightness of spirit, hope.

I am going to Dr. Ruggiero for a lengthy eye exam today. This is adding fuel to the anxiety. My MO is to approach these exams with a sense of dread. I fear that my eyes have deteriorated and I will lose my driver's license. I was uncharacteristically excited about this visit until a few days ago when fear grabbed my body and tied me in a knot of pain that left my eyes feeling dead and blind again. This scared the heck out of me.

I never again want to return to a fuzzy life. Finally I see that I have scared myself.

This I can repair.

4/25/2019 The Birth of Leaves
(on the little dog's birthday)

I haven't told anyone that I have been afraid that the miracle of my newfound sight is going away ... disappearing. Vanishing before my sad eyes, leaving me feeling distraught, isolated, alone. Stress wore at my body last week. My eyes shut down and as much as I have been giving myself over to self-care, trying to heal, relax, and rest, my eyes have not seen anything clear, brilliant, amazing for far too many days. I have been worried that the magic was gone.

Until today.

As I sat on my deck steeping in the warmth of this early Spring day, the little dog by my side, I looked at the maple tree and saw the most incredible sight.

Tiny red leaflets at the end of every single branch of that massive tree. I looked around and I saw other big maple trees with the same tiny leaves birthing on the tips of their branches.

I have never seen these delicate first signs of Spring. It is evening now and I am still smiling my biggest smile, the memory tucked safely away. Sweet celebration of the little dog's third day-of-birth.

4/27/2019 Smiling Eyes

I used to have scared eyes.

Their fear spread across my face and down into my body where I hid for a very long time.

I was always happier in small places, like my closet, feeling safe where I could reach out and touch everything , like a blind person knowing my world through my other senses.

I love using my eyes now, stretching their capacity to see and interpret the world in a way I have not known until now. I am like a baby seeing everything for the first time.

Simple things.

The new spring leaves. Following the tiny birds with my eyes as they fly to perch on a branch of the maple tree after snatching a seed from the feeder.

I am reliving a childhood of light instead of one cast in shadows. Seeing clearly has strengthened my body and soul.

4/28/2019 Going Down Stairs

When Doc Ruggeiro asked why developing depth perception was important to me I was surprised by her question, taken aback for a moment. I replied, simply " so I can walk down stairs without feeling scared."

My wish felt trivial at the time. I knew there were deeper reasons, but stair stepping was all that came to mind. I wanted to walk down a flight of stairs without fear of plummeting to the bottom in a crumpled heap of flesh and bones. Standing at the top of a flight of stairs was like looking over the edge of a cliff to nowhere. Stairs have always been a challenge -- shameless confession.

For three days now, when I walk down the splintered deck stairs to my car, I no longer need to tentatively slide my feet to each edge to make sure there is a step to descend to. I see the step is not flat but has a lovely dark edge of shadow that tells my brain and body to step down. That I will not tumble and fall. Walking down stairs is now akin to gracefully walking a red carpet, head held high. I have arrived, I am safe.

5/1/2019

Cold, damp, gray May Day.

Yesterday I saw a tree full of new Spring buds, deep burgundy, opening to a fresh light green. The tree is rooted beneath the tattered green railroad bridge that the little dog and I walk across each day on our way into town.

This was the very first crossing that I noticed the tree. The image gathers with the myriad of new pictures resting behind my eyes, filling my brain, casting light even on a day like today. I feel sunshine inside eyes that were once dark and dull.

I am always looking, trying to find hidden treasures I might have missed, no longer walking around with eyes half closed, protecting myself from the sadness and disappointment of looking for things I could not see.

As my world has opened up, I feel no longer lost but found. I wonder if I become what I see. If I only see darkness, does that leave me in a dark and lonely place, feeling light and connected only when I see outside of myself that I am not alone?

5/3/2019 Pre Dawn

Waking before dawn to a gray sky yet again, I am a bright spirit, wide-eyed. Rising up with boundless energy to greet a new day.

Where did the demons run to in the dead of night, allowing me to wake refreshed, free of darkness and dread?

I feel clean. Clear as the bright blue sky on a sunny morn. Bird song. Smell of lilacs and roses. My creation tucked deep inside the folds and wrinkles of time passed. Watching and waiting just for moments of sheer pleasure earned through so many treks in the dark, tangled jungle of memory. A life lived on back streets shrouded in hues of midnight. Streetlight glare reflecting false party face. Hiding fear of everything.

5/4/2019 Navigating Traffic

I live on the outskirts of a town of fifty thousand people where traffic is light. For me, parts of the "city" where roads have eight lanes including turn lanes, driving has the intense confusion that New York City brings to the uninitiated driver. The plain truth is that I become overwhelmed, scared out of my wits ... until yesterday.

I was headed to my most dreaded part of the "city" to run an "important" errand. I needed padded bike shorts for riding my trike, a three wheeled bike I ride due to poor balance which stems from my vision. I am headed to California where my trike lives at a friend's house near a bike path that runs along a beach where I love to ride on my west coast vacations.

When driving in congested areas, I plan a route and follow it carefully each time I need to make a trip to a particular destination. Limited sight necessitates becoming familiar with roadways over many trips, as it takes huge focus and concentration to figure out how to navigate turns and appropriate lane changes. My errand was taking me to Dick's Sporting Goods, a spot where years ago I once became "lost in space" in the middle of a huge intersection, frozen with fear, surrounded by honking cars, like a flock of angry metallic geese. I managed to maneuver out of the situation into a safe zone but the memory lingers.

Yesterday I felt no fear as I headed to Dick's to purchase my shorts. All of a sudden I realized that I was no longer driving on my usual route. Instead of freaking out I simply looked around me like a “normal” driver, saw a turn that looked promising, took several more turns and arrived at Dick’s with a huge smile on my face, a complete absence of fear.

I turned to the little dog sitting in the passenger seat, her seat belt on, and shared our good fortune. We sat for a while soaking in this moment of sweet normalcy. I left her sturdy eighteen pound self to guard our car and went about my errand.

5/5&6/2019 The Garden

I move through life differently since my eyes have become clear, steady, seeing depth. My eyes bring more of the world into focus for me to appreciate and savor.

I take my time in the garden instead of racing to the next mass of plants enmeshed with weeds, the next overcrowded family grouping, the next area to be cleared of debris to make room for freshly divided plants eager to establish their independent "digs" in the garden. I pause to look at new shoots loosely covered with Winter's clutter of damp, moldy leaves, twigs, acorns, seeds and all sorts of leavings from the forest critters who dine at my winter table, leaving an untidy mess for me to pick up and discard, clearing a place for next winter's banquet.

This morning the sun graces us with a rare visit during this soggy, gray New England Spring. The glowing yellow orb is not controlled by the calendar and knows how to tease her adoring subjects into a frenzy of delight with her brief appearances. I confess to bowing to her will, basking in her brilliance and bestowing my best smile upon the earth when she shines.

5/16/2019 Wild Sight

I feel like Dorothy on her way to OZ swept up in a swirling tornado, my body and soul tossed around, not knowing whether I am up or down, when or if I shall land, showered with spectacular images, the likes of which I have never seen.

I smile like a fool as I drive along in my car, the little dog by my side. I babble to her about the hillsides covered in soft green newly leafed trees.

Vehicles rushing by us appear to be cars from-the-future, never seen with such clarity, they become sharp-edged, glistening sci-fi wonders. Everything is exciting, no such thing as mundane scenery.

I feel like a newborn baby seeing the world for the first time. I am aware of how startling this experience is to my system and I shudder as I imagine how the babe must feel: raw, vulnerable, confused, excited, scared, lost. I feel joy, endless surprises around every "bend in the road." I try to reign in my excitement, the excess of happy tears that come unannounced at random times. I feel exposed, more vocal than my already effusive self. I am slightly worried that people who see me smiling from ear to ear for no apparent reason, laughing, crying, and chattering to myself will wonder what is going on with me.

If they ask, I shall answer that I am living heaven on earth at the moment.

5/19/2019 First Spring Paddle

I took my mini sized kayak and the little dog out on the lake yesterday for the first time this Spring. It was quite a momentous event due to the gray skies and monsoons which have drenched our region through April, into mid-May. The day was one of sparkling sunshine, cloudless blue sky, me and the little dog going to our favorite summertime spot. A half mile away from the lake my paddle partner began voicing a soft cry ... not her usual "we're at the lake let me out" ear-splitting bark. This was different, persistent, quieter. Smiling now remembering our collective joy as she bounded out of the car after I hauled my teal and white boat down to the water's edge. We climbed aboard and off we went, slowly and gently to allow the little dog to get her "sea legs" under her once again. Soon we were both settled, dressed in our safety gear: purple life jacket for me, orange jacket for the little dog. Solid strokes through the water propelled us forward while my four-legged companion sat proudly at the prow, squeaky ball in mouth ready for her first fetch and swim of the

season.

Then everything and nothing at all changed. I looked up at the woods along the shore expecting to see the usual soft green and brown collage of trees and forest floor greenery which grow along the banks of the lake. The tired old woods were gone and an Enchanted Forest had taken its place spread out all around us. The trees had sprung to life, cutting through space, cloaked in dark shadows. I felt like we were surrounded by majestic creatures who reached up into the sky , cutting through the blue, marching deep into the woods.

I realized that I was seeing the shoreline in three dimensions for the first time. The memory lingers as I write these lines, stunned into silence, sweet joy.

5/20/2019 San Diego: Second Sight

I have never seen these palm trees before, despite the fact that I have walked and ridden a trike slowly by them many times on my visits here. When did the palms grow these prehistoric scales up and down their high-in-the-sky trunks? When did they become gargantuan giants looming over me, leaving me feeling tiny, dwarfed in their presence? I stand at their feet dumbfounded, mouth wide open, amazed.

I see deeper into my world every day that I am aware, conscious and searching. These mind-states arrived with my new vision. These gifts are soul wrenching, opening my heart in ways I could not imagine. My doctor could not predict changes to my mind. I love watching her face light up when I share with her my experience. We have traveled far together and I am grateful, beyond these words, for her care and guidance on this journey.

Learning To See

I'm on vacation with my BFF in San Diego, resting my head. It is just a short trike ride to the sand and sea. A "trike" is a three wheeled bicycle which allows me, a balance challenged person, to pedal for miles on the bike path along Mission Bay, fulfilling a life-long dream -- feeling the wind and sun on my face, seeing only the ocean as I pedal along a sandy beach, purple and blue hair flying behind me. My finger-painted hair is a new addition to my colorful personality.

I have lived inland all my life, except for one year in Scituate, Massachusetts, a small sea-side town. I have spent as much time as possible walking along east and west coast beaches, tropical beaches, slogging through sand , water lapping at my toes, gazing for hours at the waves, becoming lost in their endless rhythmic water dance that calms and soothes my frenetic, cluttered mind. My secret wish has long been to feel the bliss of being at one with the waves.

My wish was granted last night when I saw the ocean in three dimensions for the first time. I was on the beach at sunset, watching the evening display of red, pink and orange streaking through the blue overhead, chatting with people, loving up sandy dogs, then solo sitting on my beach towel until there was just a touch of peach left in the sky. Knowing darkness was approaching I trudged up the beach stairs, stole one last, longing look at the water before heading home.

I was stunned by what I saw.

I had to look several times. The waves were now composed of individual ridges. I could see each individual ridge. I saw deeper, richer blues and greens, even as darkness was falling.

I was seeing ocean waves in three dimensions for the first time. I finally had the feeling of being enveloped ... merging with the water ... deep inside the waves.

When the sun disappeared, I shifted my gaze to the clouds that blanket the ocean for a night of slow dances. This evening when I turned my attention to the clouds, I noticed a monster sized cloud that hung in the middle of the night sky, inviting me to reach out and grab it in a giant bear hug The huge cloud was separate, distinct from the sky, not just a blur of fluff blended into the blue gray of night. More three dimensional sight.

This evening of amazing first sights taught me a valuable lesson. I realized that I am able to play with my vision, test out this newfound experience of seeing with depth. I noticed that when my attention wandered and I forgot to consciously focus my eyes, the ocean waves appeared flat.

My work is to harness my ability to engage my eyes in the process of seeing. Purposeful awareness, relaxing, breathing deeply, help my eyes to work together, to fuse images, see with depth perception.

I learned that I can direct my eyes to see with depth, not just wait for random experiences.

6/9/2019 Birds In The Garden

Through luck and providence, and the work of garden elves, my unruly garden has been turned into an exquisite sanctuary where fairies would be quite at home, in fact I feel like a fairy queen each time I stop and gaze at my garden from the deck, drive or garden path placed there for this purpose. I have never seen such a lovely array of meandering flowers, one that mirrors my persona, the perfect image of my "secret garden" of purples, pinks and blues, striking yet delicate, an inviting mix which drew me to plant myself in the midst of it yesterday afternoon. I pulled myself in and down to stop, to immerse myself under the late blooming Miss Kim lilac, filling myself with the scent of her huge clusters of tiny pungent lavender snifters.

And then another stunning experience. I looked at the enormous hot pink fox glove flowers towering over me, gazed deep into their bespeckled blooms, back away from typing for a moment to bask in the memory of sinking into the depth of this flower. I felt pulled inside each horn-like mouth of pink, drawn in closer than was ever possible. I stayed rooted, unable to leave. Then there arrived the dancing, flitting "jewel" of gardens in the Northeast: a male Ruby Throated hummingbird flashing red, buzzing me as perhaps an unwelcome but tolerated intruder in his garden estate. People often tell me about seeing these speedy marvels, around their flowers, not just at feeders like mine. This was a first for me, to see him in his natural habitat, I stayed on a little longer. The stopping is also new.

Hummingbirds beat their wings on average 53 times per second, creating a blur for the human eye observing this miracle. On closer inspection it is possible to see within the blur, to discern the delicate wing that moves at warp speed. I used to grab my binoculars, moving as carefully as a human can but always they detected my clumsy movements and made a speedy departure, thwarting my attempts. Even with the mechanical assist I could not see them as I am able to see them now since their Spring arrival.

Seeing these tiny visitors clearly for the first time brings on tears.

I am an almost sixty-eight year old woman skin toughened from a life spent tripping along stony pathways, now fragile, sensitive, exposed. Each new experience is a shock to my system that is just learning how to integrate a million zaps of experience.

Bluebird Bluebird, On My Window

The bluest of blue birds, an Indigo Bunting, arrived at my kitchen window sill yesterday for the first time ever. She sat there staring at me and me right back at her. Even with my "old" eyes I know I would have seen her but I would never have spotted her kin who flew around my yard throughout the morning, a family of three flitting about in the soft Spring air, one later lighting upon a window sill in the living room.

I have never been able to spot birds in trees. I have spent endless hours with birder friends who patiently tried to direct my sight to "specs" that brought so many murmured sighs of delight. Often I just lied and added my appreciative sigh to the human chorus so as not to appear "dumb" as that is how I always felt in shared "sightings" with normal sighted folks. Now I am able to spot birds without the aid of binoculars in the trees in my yard, on wires and rooftops along my walks into town with the little dog, always trotting along beside me. I also now see the hummingbirds who get their 3+ squares at my feeder daily more clearly even without binoculars. I have realized that their beaks are almost twice as long as I had perceived them to be, dagger sharp implements seeking nectar.

6/19/2019 A Snag in the Periphery

I am not seeing well lately. My newfound clarity and depth perception feels like an illusion. It has slipped away leaving me discouraged, sad, confused. The harder I try to focus and see, the worse my vision becomes. My eyes feel stressed, strained, the once beautiful countryside is now a dull blur. I finally relaxed a bit yesterday, let go of my ever present worry, stopped struggling to see, and my vision began to open up, clarity and depth perception improved just enough for me to feel hopeful that all was not lost. My peripheral vision was probably a significant factor in the change.

My vision therapist Dr Clay is teaching me to push out my peripheral vision in order to strengthen my central vision. She explained that the key to better central vision is to develop greater peripheral vision. It is counter-intuitive for me to encourage my eyes to seek out more in the periphery in order to see something directly in front of me more clearly. This crazy phenomenon works.

Yesterday in my vision therapy session, practicing an exercise used to expand peripheral vision, my sight became crystal clear once again. This reminds me that I am also better able to see with binocularity when I pay attention to the periphery. Developing peripheral vision requires intense concentration, yet the task is simply a shift in awareness. Broadening the periphery is an act of allowing my eyes to gather information, instead of fighting, grabbing, trying to gain control. Another life lesson learned from these two orbs that continue to take me into brave new worlds each day.

6/28/2019 Body Language

I have not felt at home in my own skin. I have been detached, disconnected from my flesh and bones. I have lived life through mind and emotion, body numb, frozen, sharp-edged. I presented myself as soft and welcoming to people, an unconscious deception to preserve a light spirit, a life-saving strategy.

I awoke to the realization this morning that my body has felt much the same as the paralysis brought on by Nystagmus. My eyes felt cut off from me just like my body.

I have been aware of a shift in my connection with my body for quite a while. Instead of my body being this 100 pound lump that I drag around with me, I feel physical sensations on my skin, in my muscles.

Signs of a body waking up.

I feel comfortable in my own skin. There appears to be a link between my eyes seeing clearly, with depth and my body thawing, emerging from a long sleep, a deep freeze. I feel my body waking up, coming slowly out of a cocoon, spreading fresh, damp, delicate wings. I feel a bit like an infant who first discovers her toes, sticking them in her mouth.

The change in my vision has affected the way I think. I have noticed the change gradually. People close to me have observed more clarity and insight in my thought processes. I find more creative solutions to problems. I am better able to explore "outside the box".

I am surprised by this emerging ingenuity. My mind feels clear. The fuzziness, tangled cobwebs derailing, impeding my ability to think have been replaced by a sharper mind that is able to focus, look more deeply into complex issues and situations. I do not think it is a coincidence that clear vision has opened up my mind.

I have access to more information. I can see and can read the expressions on the faces of people I encounter, allowing clearer communication.

The energy needed to navigate a blurry world of unseen hazards is now freed up to explore, create. I am physically safer now, no longer stumbling, bumping into things, frightened behind the wheel of a car.

I believe it is important not to underestimate the toll that struggling to survive took and the ease provided by clear sight.

7/2/2019 Luna

A Luna Moth is the size of a small child's hand and light chartreuse in color - exceptional size and beauty in the moth world, and quite rare. A second Luna has arrived at my house just since Summer began last week, this time alighting on my cabin wall.

I am elated, full of joy, and feel blessed when a Luna comes my way. Only one other Luna has deigned to visit in the fifteen years I have lived in my cabin in the woods.

The Luna reflects back to me the feeling I have had more and more this year of being touched by something of magic, akin to running through a field of flowers and coming upon a tiny cluster of four leaf clovers.

Brings to mind my Mom, who believed in magic, and would love seeing me see the world as I do now. This feeling of being as rare and special as a Luna has become part of my life experience, an unexpected gift. I am grateful, surprised, thrilled beyond words.

7/17/2019 Monarch

I learned the other day from my naturalist friend David that the Monarch butterfly is becoming an endangered species. They rely solely upon the Milkweed plant for their survival. The adult Monarch lays her minuscule eggs only on Milkweed, which nourishes the caterpillar which emerges from the larvae, providing sustenance to form the chrysalis. Emerging from the chrysalis, the butterfly that flies away dines on the nectar of summer flowers. I have protected a patch of milkweed from the brush hog for years, long before I knew the dear creatures were at risk.

Lately I have been walking my driveway in the early morning with the little dog, carefully looking on the undersides of leaves for the monarch's eggs which appear as a tiny white dot. David and I festooned one plant with a yellow ribbon to mark the baby caterpillar we found there. Today the caterpillar is showing off new yellow and black furry stripes.

As the little dog and I headed home up the drive I noted that I would never have had the patience to look for these tiny new born creatures before the gift of fresh new eyes. My eyes were often useless to me. I would have given up looking for Monarch eggs after one cursory peek under a leaf and that act would have been a pretense so David would not think I was too blind to see the eggs. Sadly that was the truth, until now.

A mother monarch flitted around my deck yesterday as if to thank me for keeping her nesting place safe.

I feel a connection with this butterfly I am helping to save from extinction. As my eyes evolve and I emerge into light I see the darkness in which I lived as a place where I was invisible, almost extinct. I have been saved by sight.

The End - for now

We hope you enjoyed this book. If you know someone who could be helped by Pat's experiences, please help spread the word.

Post on social media sites. Review the book on book sites.

Tell your friends.

Pat is available for interviews and talks.
Please contact her:
Pat@AnySummerSunday.com

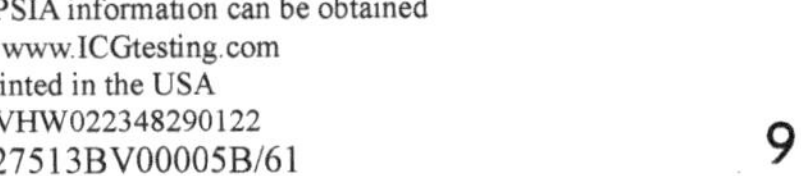

CPSIA information can be obtained
at www.ICGtesting.com
Printed in the USA
BVHW022348290122
627513BV00005B/61

9 781953 029010